FOLK COSTUMES
OF THE WORLD
IN COLOUR

DATE DUE

DEMCO 128-8155

FOLK COSTUMES OF THE WORLD.

Written by Robert Harrold

Illustrated by Phyllida Legg

BLANDFORD

First published in the U.K. 1978 by Blandford
an imprint of Cassell
Wellington House, 125 Strand
London WC2R 0BB
Reprinted 1981, 1984, 1986

This paperback edition first
published 1988
Reprinted 1989
Reprinted 1990
Reprinted 1992
Reprinted 1993
Reprinted 1994
Reprinted 1995
Copyright © 1978 and 1988 Blandford Press

Distributed in the United States by Sterling Publishing Co., Inc.
387 Park Avenue, South New York, N.Y. 10016–8810

Distributed in Australia by Capricorn Link (Australia) Pty Ltd.
2/13 Carrington Road, Castle Hill, NSW 2154

British Library Cataloguing in Publication
Data
Harrold, Roben
  Folk costumes of the world. – 2nd ed.
  1. Folk costumes to 1887
  I. Title II. Legg. Phyllics
  391',008

ISBN 0 7137 2056 5

Printed in Hong Kong by South China Printing Co.

CONTENTS

This book is dedicated to
Helen Wingrave
Fellow of the Imperial Society of Teachers of Dancing
who has done so much to promote folk dance and costume

INTRODUCTION

In recent years there has been a growing interest in folk costume, dance, song and music. Museums have been established in which to house costumes and examples of folk crafts, thus preventing them from being lost. Anthropologists and musicologists have travelled to remote villages to record folk songs and music or to notate dances. After many years of neglect, old instruments have been discovered and played again. Through this keen interest embroidery patterns and designs have been preserved and many costumes re-created.

To understand fully how folk arts developed and the influences which controlled their development, is to know a great deal of the history of a country and its people.

The basic shape evolved through the years has produced the individual costume of a country with many variations. The meaning behind so many items of clothing may well have been forgotten. The embroidery or stitching on a blouse, dress or shirt may now be merely decorative, but at one time it had a purpose or message. The wearing of a hat also had many deep and different meanings. The use of an earring or necklace could have a significance which goes back to time immemorial. People still wear their best clothes for Sundays or for religious occasions although the original purpose may well have been forgotten.

In this book the development of folk costume has been briefly outlined. Isolating the study of costume from the other folk arts can be a mistake, e.g. to understand folk dance it is important to know what the dancers wear and how the costume influences the movement. Folk music can express the characteristics of a nation, their language and history. In the long flowing phrases of Russian music there is the freedom and line of their costumes. The quick rhythm of the Ukraine is shown by the short skirts of the women. The interesting rhythms of the Balkan countries finds the dancers expressing the movement through their feet as their costumes often restrict the fuller use of the body.

Costume, dance, music, folklore and the decorative arts all reward study, but each subject is closely linked and a knowledge of them all gives a unifying and very full picture.

To give a typical example of a costume from a country is not easy as costumes change from region to region and often from village to village. Some countries have literally hundreds of costumes and a whole book could be written on one country alone.

Costumes for work differ from those worn on Sundays, high days and holidays. For the married a different dress may be worn from that worn by the unmarried or widowed. The costumes illustrated in this book are those mainly used for dancing, either by individuals or by the various national companies and groups. For example, the Scottish costume is that for a Highland dancer and not that for rural wear, and this also applies to other countries where there is a marked difference between the costume of the dancers and ordinary wear.

Many of the costumes illustrated or mentioned are now only worn by folk dance groups, at festivals or on religious occasions. They are no longer part of everyday life.

In some of the more isolated villages in Europe, Asia and in the Americas, people still wear the costumes of the region or of their tribe. It is in these areas that old costumes, superstitions and traditions are maintained.

A visit to a village wedding in one of the Balkan countries, or a journey through Turkey, Iran, North Africa, Arabia or parts of South America enables one to see a whole wealth of costume. The wearers do not regard their costumes as fancy dress; so, if reproducing costumes for a stage performance it is essential that they should be copied as accurately as possible. There is a tendency to make them more theatrical by the addition of sequins, beads, bows or other exaggerations (unfortunately some national groups do this).

If the illustrations in this book are used as a guide in the making of costumes, it is advisable to use similar colours and materials. Some of the more striking contemporary colours may look eye-catching, but cannot give an authentic impression. Fabrics with a nylon base or with a shiny and metallic surface are not ideal as they do not hang well or move with the dancer.

Although skirts have tended to become much shorter in recent years, the illustrations in this book show the typical rather than the modern. Some dance folk festivals demand authenticity and marks are lost if there is an inclination towards the theatrical.

THE DEVELOPMENT OF COSTUME

The Bible tells us that the first costumes worn by man were those devised by Adam and Eve. The aprons of leaves were followed by coats of animal skins so that they went out into the world in a costume still in use today.

As man travelled the world, his environment governed his costume. Natural resources and animal life were utilised and with man's development costume began to have a threefold purpose:

(a) As protection against the elements, insect and animal life and adapted to the requirements of the terrain,

(b) For adornment, the recognition of rank and marital status and religion.

(c) In ritual ceremonies.

All these aspects played a part in the development of costume through the ages.

Primarily a hunter, early man admired the courage and strength of the animals he killed and which provided both food and clothing. Rituals were performed by which he endeavoured to emulate these qualities by wearing their skins, and spears were ornamented with animal carvings. Religious and superstitious beliefs were linked to the wearing of special clothes.

Trees were also worshipped as a source of power and their bark and foliage were utilised in order to capture the tree spirit. The 'Tree of Life' is often depicted in embroidery. Many tribes still plait leaves to make aprons or loin cloths and the bark of trees is beaten and made into a material for clothing. In Fiji the masi, or bark cloth, is made by stripping the bark from the trees and beaten until it is paper thin. It is then joined together and dyed and made into the tapa dress.

The Aztec women still make a material called ixtle from the leaves of the maguey cactus whose tough white fibres are dyed and woven to make coarse cloth.

With the cultivation of land and the raising of cattle for food and clothing came the art of weaving. From sheep, goats, camels and llama came the wool or hair that could be utilised. In the north, the skins of caribou, reindeer, seals and the feathers and skins of birds were used. They are still used by the Lapps today. The Eskimos of the Arctic regions continue to wear all fur garments.

The Indians of North America hunted buffalo, deer, antelope, beaver and fox for their skins and fur and sinews were used for thread. With the coming of cotton, linen, wool and silk, the basic patterns were changed.

Requiring sub tropical and tropical conditions for its growth, cotton became one of the most important vegetable fibres in the world and pieces of cotton material have been found in excavations showing that it was used five thousand years ago. Cortes received the highly prized material on his arrival in Mexico. India is the most ancient cotton growing country and a system of handweaving, spinning and dyeing was in use there five centuries B.C. when Europe was still in a state of barbarism.

China also developed cotton from very early times although not on a large scale until A.D. 1300. Japan followed a similar pattern.

The manufacture of cotton was to cause radical changes in costume, especially in Europe where the material was virtually unknown. It began to be produced and flourished in Spain during the thirteenth century and later spread to the Netherlands. There is some doubt as to when the industry reached England, but it might well have been brought to England during the sixteenth century when Flemish weavers fled from Spanish persecution.

The U.S.A. did not begin the serious development of its cotton industry until the eighteenth century.

Following cotton came a whole range of fabrics for costumes. Calico, named after the city in India, became very popular. Corduroy and cambric were used extensively, as was fustian, the name being derived from El Fustat, a suburb of Cairo where the material was first made. Gingham was possibly derived from the Malaysian words ging-gang. Velveteen also came into use at this time.

Another material which came to be used extensively in making costumes was linen. The preparation and cultivation of flax was known to many ancient civilisations. In Egypt it was only the priests who were permitted to wear linen robes and it was used in the mummification of the Pharaohs. Linen, being a stronger material, had many more uses than cotton and the growing of flax was therefore important. Ropes were made from it, with the inferior material being made into tow, some of which went into the making of wicks for lamps.

Linen could be woven into a heavy material or woven into fine cambric used for shirts and blouses. Cambric as a name came from the Flemish town of Cambrai where it was first made. It could also be used in the making of lace.

The other important textile was wool, which again had its origin far back in history. It was the Romans who taught the British the arts of spinning and weaving wool and they even set up a factory for the manufacture of clothing for the occupying forces.

In Europe the wool industry flourished and the Moors introduced the famous merino strain into Spain. England benefited from the craft of the Flemish refugee weavers who settled in the country.

The Dutch introduced sheep and wool into South Africa although it did not flourish immediately.

Parts of South America, the U.S.S.R., Eastern Europe and Iceland all developed wool and incorporated it into their costumes. It became invaluable to those living in the mountains and in cold climates.

Although cotton and linen were known in many countries, silk was the product of only one country, China. Eventually, with the introduction of sericulture into Europe, silk was to play an important part in changing folk costumes. Silk is made from the cocoon of a special moth, which feeds on mulberries. In 2640 B.C. the wife of the Chinese emperor, Huang-ti, encouraged and supervised the cultivation of the mulberry tree, the rearing of the worms and the reeling of the silk. The making of the silk was a very closely guarded secret, kept by royal and noble families for many centuries; the penalty was death if the secret was divulged to others.

So prized did silk become that the famous caravan route stretching for nearly eight thousand miles from China to Rome became known as 'The Silk Road'. This route carried the precious cargo from northern China into Samarkand, Bokhara and across Persia. It continued to the Tigris and Euphrates, into Syria, Egypt and Rome. This incredible journey, with its many terrain hazards and the passing of the cargo from merchant to merchant, set silk at an enormous price.

The collapse of the Chinese dynasty in the early third century made the export of silk to the west extremely difficult. The closely guarded secrets were smuggled out of China to the outside world. Japan learnt the art from four Chinese girls. It was thought to have arrived in India with a Chinese princess who hid the eggs and mulberry seed in the lining of her headdress.

From India the making of silk slowly reached Persia and Central Asia.

Justinian the Great, the most famous of Eastern Roman emperors, was most anxious to develop the manufacture of silk and he sent two monks to China. They returned with the precious eggs hidden in a bamboo cane and thus began the first western cultivation, which started in Constantinople around 550 A.D.

The conquering Saracens carried the art as far as Sicily and eastward into Asia. The manufacture soon spread northwards to Florence, Milan, Genoa and Venice. In 1480 silk weaving began at Tours in France and forty years later in the Rhône Valley. Each country added its own particular features to colours, patterns and designs.

It was only in the sixteenth century that silk manufacture reached England, via the Low Countries and the Flemish weavers. The religious troubles in France nearly a hundred years later caused many skilled French Protestant silk workers to settle in Switzerland, Germany and England. In London the weavers settled in Spitalfields and produced a silk named after this district.

Cortes tried to introduce sericulture into Mexico and James I into America, but neither had much success and silk was to remain a product of the eastern hemisphere and, consequently, influence the costumes of that area.

THE SHAPE OF COSTUME

With the development of the basic materials, peasant costume in western Europe became established and changed only slightly from the time of the early Greeks until the fifteenth century.

The ancient civilisations of Egypt, Greece, Rome and Persia, influenced the style of dress considerably, as is shown in various articles of clothing today.

For both men and women the basic garment was a simple tunic, or chiton, made with or without sleeves. There were two kinds of garment, a short one called a Dorian tunic and a longer version known as an Ionian tunic. The latter was thought to have been introduced into Athens from Asia. The shorter tunic was more popular with the men and there were variations in style and materials used. For those working on the land the garment had a very simple cut. With the advance of civilisation the differences in the garments of the rural and social classes became more marked. Rural workers were often referred to by the Romans as Tunicati, from the simple tunica that they wore. This garment was rather like a simple shirt which reached to just above the knees or slightly higher. A form of loin cloth was worn by slaves.

Women wore the long Ionic tunic made of linen with a girdle, or zona, round the waist. The dress was made several centimetres too long and pulled up over the girdle, which gave a skirt and blouse effect. The long skirt for the women and the short Dorian style for the men was to be the basic pattern of the peasant costume until the present day.

The changes made to this style were slight, although the fashions of the social and professional classes developed and changed continuously. The long Ionic tunic introduced from the west coast of Asia Minor bears a resemblance to the present day loose fitting garments found in the Arab states of North Africa, the Middle East and Arabia.

The costumes of the social classes developed more rapidly and along different lines, governed by social status and rank. The peasant style remained unchanged as it met the requirements of the land workers.

Although trousers were not worn by the Greeks and Romans, they were in existence well before that period in history and were worn by the Asiatic nomadic and horsemen tribes. Tunics were not suitable for riding and consequently a short leather trouser evolved which gave both freedom in the saddle and when fighting on foot. This is worn today by the Turkish dancers when they perform the famous Kilic Kalkan, or sword and shield dance, dressed in early Ottoman military costumes. The Romans associated this form of costume with the barbaric civilisations on the outskirts of their empire and named the trousers after them. The Latin word was 'bracae' or 'braccae', from which we get the English 'breeches', the Scottish 'breeks', the Breton 'bragou-braz' and there are similar sounding names in other languages. With the fall of the Roman Empire trousers were adopted by men and were made of wool, linen, leather and, in the East, cotton and silk. The materials were plain, striped or decorated with various coloured wools.

Ceaseless unrest and wars brought their changes to the various civilisations and affected costume. The male tunic was to remain, but now a form of breeches, shorts or long trousers were worn underneath. The lower leg or trouser would often be bound with strips of material and eventually the binding would become part of the lacing of the boot. The next development was the tucking of the tunic into the trouser, thus becoming a shirt.

The peasant costume of the women remained the long, simply cut, one piece dress for many years. It was not until the fifteenth century, with the introduction of the bodice and the use of the apron, that the outline began to change. European changes of dress were slow and it was many years before the bodice became established. It is thought that the bodice was derived from a pattern worn by Queen Marie of Anjou in the fifteenth century and this was to vary considerably. At first it was worn over the dress and was simple in design, with either a pointed or square base. Front lacing was important. The division of the figure by the wearing of the bodice eventually led to the dress becoming a blouse and separate skirt. The bodice underwent changes, straps were added and the cut and the shape altered. It became the essential part of many European costumes and there are numerous differences even in one country or region. The blouse was also to undergo changes, with alterations to necklines and sleeve lengths according to climate, fashion or religion.

It was after the French Revolution that costume in Europe began to extend in variation and styles. Social fashions changed frequently, but the rural community was slow to change. In some parts of Europe peasants were controlled by law in the matter of dress. The laws were strictly enforced and they governed the type of material that could be used, the length of the garments, the colours and also restricted the use of decoration and trimmings. Jewellery, fancy hooks, buckles and buttons were not encouraged or elaborate dressing of the hair.

The reason for these laws was partly economic and partly religious. The Calvinistic Church feared that, without control, peasants might become extravagant in their dress or adopt fashions which could be immodest.

Governments wanted home-produced materials to be used. The social differences of the day were very marked and the upper classes did not favour peasants aping them. The French Revolution changed all this and the last of the laws were repealed. Villages vied with each other in sartorial splendour and many new ways of draping ribbons and skirts were found, with added decorations and jewellery, all bringing a wealth of new ideas.

This development coincided with the manufacture on a large scale of many new materials and designs. Many of the old ideas and traditions remained but new ideas were grafted on to them. To understand a costume fully, its history should be appreciated and the geographic features known, as all these factors have played a part in its evolution.

The difference between a working costume and one used for festive occasions is very marked. Costumes used on religious days are carefully preserved and handed down from generation to generation and are often associated with special events or traditions going back to ancient times. The animal skins and masks and the formal attire for Sundays were often thought to become impregnated either with the spirit of the animals or, indeed, the spirit of God.

EMBROIDERY, DESIGN AND PATTERN

Every country has its own folklore, legends and myths which, through the centuries, have become more elaborate and altered. Behind many of the folk stories lies profound knowledge and truth. Those unable to express in words the powers of good and evil or light and darkness, invented signs and symbols which could be understood easily. Often between ethnic groups there are similar patterns which have a universal thread linking common designs.

Man first carved patterns on stone, metal, wood and pottery and then, later, came embroidery, weaving, carpets, architecture, etc. They could be purely decorative, offer protection to the wearer or be shapes and symbols leading to more profound thoughts.

The first form of decoration was probably in the patterns that man painted upon his body and the colours used—red, blue, yellow and white—were to represent earth, air, fire and water. The designs, apart from being for protection, also had tribal meanings. With the development of clothes, patterns were transferred to materials. Superstition and the belief in the power of evil led to cosmic symbols being used wherever there was an opening in a garment. Embroidery was used round the neck and openings in shirts and blouses; cuffs, edges of sleeves and hems were all protected with decorative symbols. As man moved further away from these original intentions he became more superstitious and embroidery was placed along the seams, on the tops of stockings, knitted into socks, bound round the head on braid or material and used on veils and hats. Today these features are still evident, for example, in Lapland where the colours and designs have kept their simplicity: when embroidery was not used the edge of the garment was left fringed, later followed by lace.

One of the oldest of man's symbols has been the circle and interlocking spiral, which can be traced from the Stone Age and ancient China into Celtic patterns, as well as maori tattoos and Islamic arabesques.

The circle represented perfection, completeness, unity and the Creator. The spiral or labyrinth design represents man's rebirth into life and the path from the world towards the divine.

Apart from the circle and labyrinth, there was the triangle, an ancient symbol with cosmic and religious significance. Throughout the years these symbols became embellished with many decorative patterns.

17

Many of the old designs can still be seen, but others have changed completely. The circle became a sun, wheel or flower, the spiral became a serpent, triangles became stars and the 'Tree of Life' carried many motifs.

With the passing of the years, stitchcraft took on powerful meanings: there was a significance in whether the stitches passed from left to right or east to west. The cross, used both in stitching and design, represented the four cardinal points of the world with the fifth point being the vertical direction arising from the centre. Known as the cosmic quadrangle, it was an important symbol of life.

Each country developed its own individual designs and within a country each region, village and valley had variations. Many of the old designs have been preserved as families have passed them down from generation to generation, but other patterns have changed with the passing of time.

Patterns began to reflect environment and were incorporated into the older designs. Embroidery and costume became a form of identity revealing country, region and even village and trade.

Symbols are closely linked to the great religions of the world and the religious factor had a great influence on designs: Islamic religion forbade the reproduction of living creatures and so a very elaborate form of patterns developed. Stylised animals appeared in many countries and scorpions and spiders were used as warning symbols.

Colours played an important part in costume and embroidery. Dyes such as yellow came from saffron, the stamen of the crocus, vine leaves and the rinds of pomegranates. Red came from madder together with kermes, or cochineal, an insect found in the kermes oak or in cacti: blue came from the indigo plant. The roots, stalks, seeds and fruits were all utilised in many ingenious ways. The depth of colour was controlled by the type of water used, e.g. rain, river or spring. The time of the year in which the plant was harvested also affected the colour, as did the quality of the soil. Vegetable dyes proved to have a richer and more natural colour, but these became lost with the introduction of aniline and other chemical dyes.

Colours came to have different meanings in different countries: for example, in Europe and America black denotes mourning, but in China white is associated with grief. The Syrians and Armenians wear light blue for mourning, in the Far East yellow is used and in Iran the colour is that of withered leaves.

Red is a very popular colour as it expressed happiness, life and love, and it is also worn as a protective charm: many necklaces are made of red beads or coral. In Italy and Sicily pieces of coral tied round the neck with red braid were worn by children and the necklace was called a bulla by the Romans.

In other countries blue beads are worn for the same reason. Metal was also supposed to have special powers and small mirrors and sequins were incorporated into patterns to ward off evil spirits. Metal thread was used for the same reason. Metal was also considered to contain very special powers and necklaces, earrings, bracelets, rings, clasps on belts and the circling of metal belts had the same properties and intentions as embroidery. Stones were also believed to possess magic powers and were made into necklaces and sewn onto costumes. They were passed from generation to generation and were symbols of self being complete, unchanging and lasting.

THE HAT

In many civilisations the head was considered to be the seat of power as well as the highest point of man's body. Many religious traditions, legends and rituals have developed round this idea. This very sensitive and vulnerable part of the body has always required some form of protection. The hat developed with a three-fold purpose: it offered protection from the elements, it became a sign of status and it was used for rituals.

Early man used animal skins incorporating these three ideas. The skins not only provided covering for the body and the head, but it was believed that from these a vital force could be inherited and that this power would enable the wearers to become more efficient as hunters and gain control over animals.

The horns and other parts of the animal were used as decoration. A hat made of skin is still worn by those who depend upon hunting for their livelihood.

In many countries the shepherds still wear sheepskin hats and jackets, and the hats range from neat round ones to the large shaggy types, as well as knitted woollen caps. The wearing of animal heads at carnivals stems from these old traditions.

The feathers of birds were also used extensively for head-dresses. The feathers of the eagle were very popular in many countries where this bird was greatly revered and looked upon as a symbol of power and strength. North American Indians also used them to denote rank and bravery as well as power. During their ceremonies, plumes symbolised the carrying of prayers upwards in the same way as lighted candles do in religious ceremonies.

Various tribes in Africa and South America, as well as those in the Pacific, have beautiful head-dresses made entirely of feathers, and are so designed to give a halo effect, thus glorifying the head.

In Europe feathers are sometimes worn on the side of a hat.

Tree worship was expressed by the use of foliage in the making of a head-dress. Floral crowns and wreaths show the links associated with the various deities of the earth and of fertility. Flowers had special meanings, as with the use of colours, and they were carefully blended according to the season of the year or the occasion. Many floral head-dresses are still worn but others have been replaced by floral posies which can be used on either men's or women's hats.

Hats were linked with the creation by the people of Asia in the making of hats with plaited straw or rushes. These give protection from both the sun and rain and can be seen in China, Japan and the Far East, and the shape has only changed slightly throughout the years.

As man developed and tribes gradually migrated to other environments, the use of fur was not always practical and this led to the making of felt through the matting of fur. This material is thought to be one of the oldest invented, even preceding the weaving of wool and cotton.

The first type of hat in Europe was probably round, fitting well onto the head like a skull cap and made of felt. In Greece and Rome this was known as a petasus or pileus and is still worn in the Arab States. The skull cap also represented liberty and when a Roman slave obtained his freedom, his head was shaved and he was allowed to wear the pileus. The skull cap was also worn by the Celts. Gradually a shallow brim was added to the crown and the hat became similar to that depicted worn by Mercury and Hermes. The brim was for added protection against the sun.

The hat began to be linked with position or trade and a type of cap was evolved for sea-faring men: Ulysses is often shown wearing one of these.

From Persia came the Phrygian bonnet, a hat which originated in Asia Minor and the East, and which became the basis of many styles. Originally it was worn by the Persian soldiers and was a short pointed, conical shaped hat much favoured by the god Mithras. His religious influence brought it to England and well might have been responsible for the appearance of the Saxon type of hat with which it had much in common.

The hats of the peasants remained simple and were adapted for their work or trade. Many countries had strict sumptuary laws which clearly defined what they could and could not wear. When these laws began to be repealed the women copied some of the court styles. Christianity had demanded codes of dress and uncovered heads for women, particularly in church, were forbidden. They were expected to wear a wimple at all times and this is reflected in the general use of headscarves. The covering of the head became an essential part of peasant costume and different types of head covering for married or unmarried women were evolved.

In the fifteenth and sixteenth centuries in France and the Flemish countries, the relaxing of the laws regulating costume coincided with the growth of the lace-making industry. Hats and head-dresses appeared made of starched cotton and lace. Many of these were not practicable for work, but were worn on Sundays. It was during this period that many new head-dresses were designed.

Climate also played its part in the shaping of a hat. In the colder countries sheepskin and other fur was generally used: in Tibet, ear flaps were devised, a style also found in other countries.

In hot climates, hats with wide brims were necessary and the horsemen of North and South America, Mexico, Spain and the Hungarian Plains all wore hats with wide brims.

Straw hats in various shapes and sizes were found from the Far East to the Americas and were worn both by men and women. In Portugal a small felt hat is worn by the women which gives shade to the eyes, but no protection to the neck. A headscarf is draped over the head and then the hat placed on top: this style is also found in the Canary Islands.

In Italy the women wear draped and folded material to protect their heads and in other countries there are capes, mantillas or wimples for head wear.

In countries where the women carry large water jars or baskets on their heads, they have flat pads (sometimes known as mother-in-laws).

Countries which came under the Ottoman Empire adopted the Turkish custom of veiling and veils are worn in many of the Balkan countries. Turbans, fez or the draped kaffiyeh are worn by men of the Islamic faith and these have a religious significance as well as acting as a protection against the weather. Turbans are a protection against the sands of the desert and the Tuareg men of the southern Sahara wear turbans with veils, similar in type to the turban style of hat worn by the women of Fano, Denmark. This hat has a mask which covers the lower half of the face and acts as a protection against the sand whipped up from the dunes.

In parts of Yugoslavia and Albania the men wear a turban which also wraps round the neck and this is a protection against the cold in winter and the heat in summer.

Many factors have gone into the shaping of hats and headdresses, for example, the discarded hats of Napoleon's army in retreat influenced those in Austria. Another example is the wearing of a baby's christening robe on the head, as is found in Mexico.

The hat or head-dress also denoted rank: that worn by the head of a tribe differed from the rest. Head coverings and colours also changed within the regions of a country: special hats were used for funerals, festive occasions, Sundays, winter and summer. There was a marked difference between the hats of the married and unmarried women, as well as between village and village or tribes.

SHOES

In comparison with other items of clothing, shoes have changed very little over the years. In social circles shoes went through every conceivable style and shape, although these changes did not affect the rural worker. For the land, a tougher and long lasting shoe was essential; once this was established it remained unaffected by fashion. Shoes were expensive to buy and were not easily made in the home, unlike other articles of clothing which could be woven and stitched together; shoes required the instruments of the shoemaker's craft. Peasants found a simple design that was economical and practical.

Early settlers wore no shoes and for many this is still ideal and a solution to the problem. In some countries it is not unusual to find country people walking for miles barefooted and putting on shoes just before they enter a town.

A very early Egyptian drawing depicts a nobleman walking barefooted followed by a servant carrying his shoes in readiness for when they would be required. At one time shoes were a status symbol and peasants and slaves were not encouraged to emulate their masters. It was also considered effeminate for men in some countries to wear sandals. Slaves were often kept shoeless in order to prevent escape.

One of the earliest forms of shoe or sandal was probably made from woven palm leaves, papyrus or vegetable fibre. The design was very simple and the shoe was kept in place by bands of linen or leather thongs.

Various names were given to the earlier form of shoe, one being the Latin solea from which comes the English word sole. The rope soled, canvas topped alpargatas of Spain, the espadrilles of France, the ciocie of Italy (from the Latin sicyonia) and the ushutas of South America all have their origins in the simple type of shoe produced by the Roman civilisation.

Another type of peasant sandal which has survived through the centuries is the flat sole which is kept in place by two straps. This form of footwear has its present day counterpart in the Japanese geta or zori and the sandals of Arabia, North Africa and parts of South America. The early Greek actors and comedians wore a light pull-on shoe or slipper called a soccus, from which comes the word sock. Eventually the soccus, which was made from soft leather or wool, had a division between the first and second toes and was worn by the more privileged person and was another form of flat sandal. It was the forerunner of the Japanese tabi or jak tabi, the worker's shoe.

One of the basic peasant shoes was made from animal skin and a piece of leather was bound to the foot with cross thonging. Sometimes the lacing was tied round the ankle or it was criss-crossed round the lower leg or trouser. There are numerous examples of this type of shoe to be found, from that of the Scottish ghillie, the mountaineer's shoe from Poland to those of the Balkan countries. In many of these shoes a pronounced turned-up shoe is found and this developed from the thonging of the leather which caused the end to curl slightly upwards. It was also a protection for the toes against rough ground or stones.

In early days the use of animal skins for shoes followed the same superstitious belief associated with the use of skins for clothing, i.e., that the speed, courage and strength of the dead animal would be transmitted to the wearer.

A form of moccasin was worn by the North American Indians and these varied according to the climate. Those who settled in the Arctic regions wrapped sealskin round the legs and a type of fur boot evolved. This is also found with the Lapps, in Greenland and those living in Siberia. The fur is often worn inside for greater warmth, as with slippers. In warmer regions, the fur was removed and only the skin used.

Wood was a material that was not used extensively for footwear although occasionally a sole was made from it. Wood lacked pliability and thus restricted the movement of the foot.

Wooden soles were once strapped to the feet of Roman prisoners, making any form of escape difficult. The wooden sabot or clog developed from the high wooden pattens worn by ladies of fashion to protect their shoes from the muddy streets of the sixteenth, seventeenth and eighteenth centuries. The peasants wore a patten called a galoche, which originated in the Ardennes and which had wooden soles, but leather tops. The wooden shoe proved to be serviceable and popular in the Low Countries and France, as they kept the feet dry and were hardwearing. They were made from willow, poplar or any strong wood which did not split. They were generally used in flat countries: mountain people required a shoe which enabled them to grip a rough surface.

A clog makers guild was formed in the Netherlands in 1570 and this type of footwear is still used in some areas of the country to the present day. It did not appear in England until a much later date and became popular with the millworkers in the north during the nineteenth century. Clogs and sabots are essentially work shoes and were replaced on Sundays or other festive occasions with leather shoes, often with a silver buckle and in a style copied from those of the eighteenth century.

The other form of peasant footwear was the boot and this developed to give necessary protection round the calf and ankle. Thorns, animal bites and the chafing of horse riding, as well as cold weather and snow called for the protection of the lower leg by using skins, leather, and bark of trees, cloth, metal coverings and even rings. In time the leggings became attached to the shoe, although there was always the alternative of using them separately.

The boot was known in ancient civilisations and was particularly popular among soldiers, with red as a predominant colour as it absorbed the bloodstains from the toes, a result of arduous training. With the development of military uniforms, this colour was replaced by black. The popularity of the boot was carried through Europe by a succession of invading armies and, in particular, by the skilled horsemen. Cowboys and other horsemen adopted the boot as essential wear and in countries such as Poland, Hungary and the U.S.S.R., with their military and equine backgrounds, it was worn by the peasantry.

ICELAND

Iceland, a country of waterfalls, volcanoes, green valleys and hot geysers, has gained fame for its literature, especially the sagas and skaldic poetry which developed and flourished in the thirteenth century. The main folk activity has always been song rather than dance, with its close link to the literary background; another reason is that the island lacks trees or the natural materials for making musical instruments to provide a background for dancing.

Apart from the main industry of fishing, Iceland has over two million sheep. Thus, wool is naturally used extensively for clothing, being both warm and protective. Unlike other northern countries, who favour light colours, the Icelanders have the proclivity for using black; this may be because they do not have natural resources for making dyes.

Older women wear long, full, black skirts with a black bodice with sleeves. The bodice is either laced up with gold cord or with two gold buttons and a gold brooch, and it is decorated with gold and green embroidery. Patterns circle the skirt at about calf height and decorate the hem. Designs are usually of leaves and the curving motif shows the Celtic background combined with the Viking love of gold.

A white or coloured blouse is worn under the bodice and a gold linked chain belt worn at the waist. Some of the younger girls wear sleeveless bodices, black skirts and a full apron of blue or checked material.

Head-dresses are unusual in design. A gold band fits round a small white hat with a curled crown, rather like the Phrygian style hat, and over this a fine white veil is draped. The hair is often dressed in two plaits which are looped up and caught at the back or left to hang down either side. A firm leather shoe is worn.

In Plate 1 the woman on the left wears the more elaborate 'ceremonial' version of this costume; the head-dress is unusual and is an old style now rarely seen. The bunch of keys hanging from her belt indicates her marital status. The other woman, dressed in a work costume, wears a black velvet skull cap; the long black tassel on the right side is fixed to the cap with two or three inches of gold rings.

The men wear black breeches, a high cut waistcoat and a jacket with many silver buttons as a decorative relief. Leather gaiters are worn over stout shoes and a woollen skull cap provides protection against the weather.

LAPLAND

Lapland is the home of the Lapps, or Samek as they prefer to be called. These nomadic people, who follow the reindeer herds, have a highly developed culture, adapted to their way of life and the hardship of living in sub-zero temperatures.

The whole of life centres round the reindeer, which is used for food, clothing, trading and transport, the animals being harnessed to sledges; even the gut is used for sewing skins together.

Their costumes, like their way of life, has hardly altered over the years. In winter both sexes wear tunics and trousers made from reindeer skins, usually with the hair worn inside for added warmth. Underneath the outer garments are woollen shirts and jumpers to give further protection. Reindeer skin boots are worn in the winter; the insides are often padded with a type of rush grass which helps to keep the feet warm. The boots are made from the leg or head skin of the reindeer, this having a greater thermal value.

In the summer the fur tunics and trousers are exchanged for a similar type of garment made of wool and usually blue in colour, and moccasins with a slightly turned up toe are worn.

Red and yellow patterned braid is used for decoration and this is placed round the neck, down the front, on all the seams and around the hem of the tunic. The use of braid follows the old custom of warding off evil spirits.

It is interesting to note that, due to their isolation, the Lapp costume is a perfect example of the type of basic garment worn by most races in Europe. The remoteness of the country has not exposed its inhabitants to the fashionable influences of other countries.

A very colourful part of the Lapp costume, especially for men, is a blue cap with a large red pom-pom on top. A cap, older in origin but not always worn now, is the cap with a crown of four points. This is known as the 'cap of the four winds' (Plate 2). From the headband a knot of coloured ribbons is fixed and if the wearer places the points all facing front, it denotes that he is unmarried. The cap had originally a square crown, but the four corners were gradually pulled out making it into four points. The crown is stuffed with down or reindeer hair. There are several variations of headdress and these differ with the area.

Both men and women wear a tunic, but that of the woman is slightly longer and she wears a red woollen bonnet. In the summer the bonnet is edged with lace and a bright apron and shawl are also worn.

Over their tunics they wear a wide leather belt studded with silver ornaments and fastened with a silver clasp. A knife is usually fixed into the belt, an essential piece of equipment for the Lapp.

Both sexes wear thick mittens and there is an old tradition that when a man wished to court a girl he would try and pull a mitten off her hand, which she allowed if she agreed.

Plate 2 shows the different styles of costume found in Lapland.

FINLAND

Finland, or Suomi as it is called in Finnish, is bounded on the west by Sweden and on the east by the U.S.S.R.

Over the past 800 years the country has been ruled by Denmark, Sweden and Russia, but the Swedish influence has been the greatest as their sovereignty lasted over 600 years. It was only in 1917 that Finland became an independent State. Possibly because of their long history of occupation, the Finns have developed a reserved approach to life and to other people and this quality is reflected in their dances and costumes, which reflect an inherent dignity.

As in most northern countries, Midsummer's Eve is celebrated with bonfires, music and dancing and is an event not to be missed after the long, dark and cold winter. The value attached to the summer months is shown in the use of colours for their costumes: yellows, blues, reds, greens and white . . . all of which reflect the sun, summer skies, flowers, grass and the forests and lakes for which Finland is famed.

The costumes are simple, but very attractive, often made of vertically striped material. Skirts are fairly long and are heavy, suitable for a country with such a rigorous climate demanding added protection against the cold. Bodices and skirts made of the same striped material are very popular, and there are variations in their wear, such as a striped bodice with plain skirt or vice versa. The bodices, which are always sleeveless, can be laced up the front, fastened with two, three or four silver buttons, caught with a silver clasp or crossed over and fastened with two rows of buttons. A white apron is sometimes worn, either plain or embroidered, and a white blouse with long full sleeves and a high neck ending in a little frill, a round edge or a small collar. A loose pocket, similar to those of Sweden and Norway and showing individual variations in embroidery, is fastened at the waist. A round silver brooch of traditional design, often reflecting sun worship and a legacy from the Viking and Nordic races, is pinned on to the blouse or, alternatively, a silver chain necklace is worn. Jewellery is passed down through the generations and the men's silver or brass buttons also pass from generation to generation.

The head-dress consists of a little cap edged with lace and with a bow fixed at the back. In some areas these bows have long ends. Young girls tie a ribbon round their hair and let the long ribbon ends hang down the back. White or red stockings are usually worn with silver-buckled black shoes.

Cotton has been used for many items of clothing since the nineteenth century, when a Scotsman, James Finlayson, started a cotton mill in Tampere.

The men's costumes, which show more Swedish influence than those of the women, are sober—black or dark blue breeches or trousers, with a jacket to match, worn with a double-breasted waistcoat, striped and fastened with two rows of silver or brass buttons. The shirt is white with a stand-up collar, fastened at the neck with a silver brooch. White or dark red socks are worn and either a skull cap or a felt hat. Black shoes with silver buckles are most commonly used.

Plate 3 illustrates the basic simplicity of the Finnish costume. Both women wear bodices of popular design. The woman wearing the red bodice (from the west of Finland) is married, denoted by leaving the top two buttons undone, and her lace-edged bonnet is also an indication of married status. The girl in green wears a costume from the south-west; she is unmarried and wears a ribbon in her hair, in the style of young girls and children.

The costume of the man on the right, from Askola near Helsinki, shows strong Swedish influence. The man carrying the large black felt hat wears an older style costume from Kaukola. His moccasin-type shoe is similar to those worn in the summer by the Lapps.

NORWAY

Although Scandinavian countries share much in common, each country has developed its own folklore, costumes and dances. In spite of five hundred years of domination, only achieving independence in 1814, the Norwegians have preserved their own traditions. Midsummer Day is celebrated all over the country with bonfires and replaces the old pagan festival held in honour of the sun, or solsnu, and there are many customs and stories relating to trolls, giants, mermen, mermaids and water spirits.

The costumes throughout Norway are extremely attractive, with many marked differences from those of neighouring countries. The difficult terrain, of mountains, fjords and forests, together with the climate has kept travel to a minimum within the country and has led to a very individual development of costume in each area. Through the long dark winters, materials were woven and dyed, garments embroidered and stockings knitted. Old Viking patterns were used, but the embroidery on the bodice or skirt hem reveals the wearer's region. The designs are often geometrical with shapes reminiscent of enlarged snow crystals.

The length of the women's skirts varies from long, calf or ankle length to the fairly short double skirt of Setesdal. The skirts allow dancers to move freely and steps are executed with a lilting quality. Black skirts with a red bodice embroidered with tiny white beads and a white apron showing intricate drawn thread work are worn at Voss (Plate 4). The costume from Setesdal has a double flared skirt with stiffened bands of red and green at the hem, which make the skirt stand out. In Hallingdal, a valley north-west of Oslo, the women's skirts have a medieval line, the fullness coming from a very high cut bodice with no waistline. A white long-sleeved blouse is worn with most costumes and this is caught at the neck with a silver brooch. Beaten silver and gold jewellery is worn a great deal and again the designs reflect Viking ancestry. In western Telemark, on her wedding day, a girl is given a large brooch, usually an heirloom, representing the sun.

Unlike Denmark and Sweden, where the bodices are mostly plain, Norway favours bodices embroidered on the sides, round the edges or on a central panel. The motif, especially in the central and eastern areas, is of baroque acanthus leaves worked in coloured wools.

On the west coast many of the costumes have loose pockets or bags, attached to the belts by silver hooks. Head-dresses are simple, married women usually tucking their hair away, unmarried women wearing little caps or bonnets which are tied under the chin or, alternatively just a band round the head. Unmarried women and young girls from Voss (Plate 4) wear either a little red bonnet embroidered on the sides or are bareheaded. Married women wear a specially folded white headscarf. Stockings are usually black and silver-buckled shoes are worn.

The men wear black breeches tied below the knees with coloured braid. Waistcoats can be black, red or green and are fastened with a double row of silver or brass buttons. Short jackets are worn and in Telemark the jacket is white with black wool embroidery, worn over a white shirt, black waistcoat and breeches. Plate 4 illustrates a costume from this region. Two filigree buttons also fasten the stand-up collar of the shirt, and the coat collar, breeches and buckled shoes show the influence of the eighteenth century. The white stockings are knitted in a special pattern.

An unusual costume comes from Setesdal, where the men wear a type of dungaree with a short jacket embroidered in red, yellow and green.

It is thought that in the past many Norwegian men became mercenary soldiers and brought back other ideas from abroad; for example, the leather on the trousers in the Setesdal costume is thought to be based on the pattern of the uniform of the Spanish cavalry.

SWEDEN

Sweden is the largest of the Scandinavian countries and in common with her neighbours, Norway and Denmark, her early history follows a similar pattern of Viking domination.

Festivals are held to celebrate the light and sun, one of the most popular being Midsummer Eve. Maypoles are decorated with green branches and flowers, and dancing continues through a night which has no darkness, being so far north. In the province Dalarna, 'the heart of Sweden', this festival is particularly colourful, with everyone wearing national costume and dancing traditional dances. The other important festival is that on Walpurgis Eve, April 30th when bonfires are lit to celebrate the advent of spring following the long dark days of winter.

Swedish costumes are simpler in style than those of Denmark. The skirts are not as long or as heavy, allowing for greater freedom of movement, as well as precision in the dance steps. They are usually plain in colour, either blue, red, green, yellow or black, chosen to reflect the colours of the countryside as well as the seasons.

The bodice or corselet is usually laced up at the front and worn over a white long-sleeved blouse. The lacing on the bodice passes through eyelets made of silver or pewter.

Each region has its own type of apron or costume. Aprons can be either plain, with perpendicular stripes, horizontal stripes or plain with horizontal stripes at the bottom only; alternatively, they can be flowered, checked or plain white. In Stockholm, blue is worn, a colour which is very popular in Sweden, and also used extensively in Finland and Lapland. Newly married women or newcomers to a parish are expected to conform to the costume of that village.

The head-dress is fairly simple, consisting of various kinds of bonnets or caps which turn up at the back. In some areas unmarried girls wear red bonnets and the married women wear white. Married women are not expected to show their hair, so it was tucked away into the bonnet, or a cap or white fine material was worn under the headdress.

Shawls are worn with many of the costumes and in Stockholm these are bright red, patterned with flowers with a red fringed edge. The shawl is worn rather like a cape, fastened in front with a brooch. In Värmland the shawl is white, decorated on the edge with a red design and is similar to a large white collar. The girls in Östergötland wear a similar shawl, but tuck the front ends into the waistband. At Leksand, in Dalarna, the shawl is white patterned with red roses and the same material is used to make a tight fitting bonnet.

Many costumes have braid belts which are knotted at the side with the long ends, complete with tassels, hanging down free. The problem of having no pockets is resolved by the wearing of a type of reticule or aumônière. This is a flat bag, either square or oval in shape and embroidered with bright coloured wools; it is suspended from the waistband by a coloured braid, usually from the left hip. This type of pocket or pouch has been in use since Greek and Roman times. Red stockings are usually worn with black shoes.

The man's costume is similar to those found in other Scandinavian countries; yellow or dark blue breeches fastened below the knee with red braid and pom-poms. The waistcoat can be red or striped and is fastened down the front with metal buttons. A white shirt, white or blue stockings and black shoes with brass or silver buckles complete the costume. A type of skull cap in red, blue or black and decorated with red, yellow or black braid, or in some regions a top hat or a woollen Phrygian style cap is worn.

All the costumes illustrated in Plate 5 come from the area round Stockholm, and show the outline on which many other regional costumes are based.

DENMARK

Denmark is the smallest of the Scandinavian countries, but at one time it was the most powerful and was the cultural centre of the Nordic race. The Reformation in Scandinavia, however, had a sobering effect, both on costume and dance. Many of the old dances lapsed and peasant dress became very conservative.

Costumes are still worn on some of the islands and in coastal areas by the fisherfolk. Women favour rather long and somewhat heavy skirts, either gathered or pleated; the skirt is full, allowing plenty of room for movement, but length and weight gives a heavy quality to dancing.

Peasants usually wove their own materials from wool and used simple designs. Affluent farmers' wives and townspeople would, on special occasions, wear silk which often had accordion pleats. The dress from Amager, originally used for church-going, has a red pleated skirt edged with a black border. Pleats were formed by hand—first the skirt was dampened, then the pleats were pressed in, and the skirt was wrapped in a muslin cloth and put in an oven to dry. This process was known as 'cooked' pleating.

The most popular colours are green, red and yellow, representing the colours of the landscape and seasons. Many costumes have bodices and skirts of the same colour and material, but there are many variations, such as red stripes on a dark background worn with a blue bodice, or fine yellow stripes on red worn with a red top. Colour also reveals marital status: in Fano, red skirts are worn by married and older women and myrtle green by the young ones.

An unusual feature is for the sleeveless bodice to be worn over a blouse or dress of contrasting colour. A costume from Mols shows a dark blue bodice worn with long red sleeves: a similar costume from the Praestoe area has a red and green striped bodice edged with green and worn with red three-quarter length sleeves.

Large aprons, reaching nearly to the hem of the skirt, are found in most areas. Some are so large they resemble a skirt. A check pattern is very popular; the checks can be large or small and vary in colour. A costume worn in Roemeo shows green and yellow checks on a dark background and worn over a red skirt. White aprons with a drawn thread design, embroidered in white or patterned, are also popular; the aprons are made of cotton, but silk is used for special occasions.

32

The head-dress is based on a simple form of bonnet, often in a plain material; married women wear black or dark colours and young girls wear white. In the Medebo region, a coloured scarf is tied over the bonnet. At Fano, on the north sea coast, a curious mask is worn as a protection against the sand whipped up by the gales.

Small check-patterned shawls are sometimes worn. Red checks on a navy background signify joy, but blue or green checks on navy are a sign of mourning.

The men wear breeches caught below the knees with bands and tassels; colours are yellow, white or black, according to the district. Striped waistcoats decorated with silver buttons are worn and if a man wears a yellow silk waistcoat, it signifies that he has crossed the equator. A jacket can be worn with this waistcoat, likewise decorated with silver buttons. Under the waistcoat is worn a white shirt with a stand-up collar around which is knotted a colourful handkerchief. A red stocking cap with a tassel is popular as headgear.

Both sexes wear black shoes with silver buckles.

Plate 6 illustrates three Danish regional costumes. The young woman in red wears a country style dress from Odense. Over a red woollen blouse she has a sleeveless bodice edged with gold braid. Her checked apron is made of cotton. The head-dress is made in two sections—a style often found in Denmark. The white, tight fitting under-bonnet is made of fine cotton and the two side folds tie under the chin; on the back of the head is a small red half-bonnet edged with braid and decorated at the back with a bow. This little bonnet is also tied under the chin. Although this rather Puritan style covers the hair, the use of white shows that the lady is unmarried.

The more elaborate dark costume (right) comes from Falster. This costume is worn by married women, the material being darker and the bonnet partially covering the face. This costume would be used for such occasions as attending church on Sundays. The bodice and cuffs have bands of mauve embroidered silk which are sewn on to the material and then edged with braid. The under-sleeves in printed cotton are gathered at the wrists and partly cover the hands. The black silk skirt is hidden by a large striped apron. A scarf is tied round the neck. The large white bonnet is made of starched cotton or linen and edged with lace; it is fastened on to a black half-bonnet with a blue ribbon at the back and tied under the chin.

The man comes from the coastal area in east Jutland and wears the typical yellow breeches seen in Denmark and Sweden. The striped jacket is buttoned to the neck, and a coloured handkerchief is tied in a knot around the neck. This was a working costume, so the buttons are plain rather than silver. He wears the red woollen fisherman's hat common to seafaring people in many parts of Europe.

THE NETHERLANDS

The national character of the Dutch people is reflected in their costumes which show considerable differences between regions and even villages. Many are still worn whilst others only appear at festival times or on other special occasions. A costume can reveal the religion and marital status of the wearer, social position and whether from an agricultural or fishing background; it can also show mourning.

The skirts are usually made of heavy home-spun black wool, under which several heavy petticoats are worn to keep out the cold. Red was at one time the most popular colour for the petticoats and the skirts are full, allowing for freedom of movement when working outdoors. There is a great contrast between the sombre clothes worn for work and the garments worn on Sundays or festive occasions. In some regions costumes change from winter to summer when lighter skirts are worn. Striped material is very popular and is used for aprons and skirts. Aprons can be plain, however, as in the fishing village of Scheveningen, where black silk is worn for Sundays and blue cotton for weekdays.

In Staphorst aprons are black with an upper border of pink or white check material. Other regions reverse the designs, having a check lower section and a plain coloured border, or the apron is checked with no border.

There are several types of bodices, which are usually sleeveless and cut with a round high neck. Known as a 'tight wrap', they are worn over a vest with long or elbow length sleeves. In Marken the tight wrap has a flowered pattern embroidered in coloured wools, two roses from the age of six to sixteen, and fastened at the back: from sixteen onwards, five roses and a front fastening: for a bride there are seven roses. The undervest or sleeves are of red and white stripes. In some areas a jacket is worn over the tight wrap, either buttoned to the neck or with an open neck line. Shawls are of lace, wool, silk or a checked material, of various sizes, and are worn in a variety of ways. The Burghers' costume from Friesland is particularly attractive—the dresses are made of patterned silk with a white lace fichu or shawl and apron, together with a châtelaine bag hanging from a belt.

One of the most interesting aspects of the women's costumes are the numerous head caps. The custom of wearing a cap developed from the days when they were worn in the house. The caps vary from two or three separate sections up to twelve; they are worn over a type of head-clip or head band which holds and supports the complicated lace and pleated material. The bands are made of gold and usually end in an ornament. Gold pins fasten the band to the cap and these can also end in square, oval or spiral shapes. Sometimes the metal decoration protrudes from under the cap and lies on the forehead or flat against the cheeks. Round discs signify the Catholic religion, squares denote Protestants. Two, three or four rows of coral beads, fastening with a gold clip at the front or back, are worn with most costumes. Coral is regarded as lucky.

Black stockings are worn with most costumes, apart from those of the Burghers from Friesland where white stockings are worn.

Men's costumes are far less complicated. Fishermen wear wide, black, baggy trousers, the fullness allowing plenty of freedom for working on the boats. These trousers are modelled on those worn by seventeenth century seamen. The men of Urk wear wide trousers which end just below the knee and are similar to knickerbockers, or the bragou braz of the Breton sailors.

A similar type of trouser is worn on the Island of Marken, but they are slightly shorter and are white in summer and black in winter: black stockings are worn. Fishermen wear either a shaggy cap or sometimes a hat; farmers are distinguished by less baggy trousers and by a peaked cap. Trousers are usually fastened in front with a flap and two buttons, often made of silver. Long-sleeved, double breasted and collarless jackets, fastening up to the neck with two rows of silver buttons, are worn in many areas. In Staphorst the working jacket is dark blue and tucked into the trousers, with white braces over the top.

Shirts are long-sleeved and fastened at the neck with two silver or gold collar studs. Blue and white stripes are popular, especially for weekdays, with a change to black or a dark colour for Sundays. A knotted tie is worn under the front studs and the colour can denote mourning, with black and white for half mourning. At one time a silver watch and chain was worn; if the chain was worn horizontally it conveyed that the wearer was married, but if left to dangle, signified a bachelor.

In Marken boys and girls are dressed alike in skirts up to the age of six, but small details denote the sex of the child. The boys have studs in their collars and horizontal slit pockets in their skirts, whereas the girls have vertical pockets. There are also slight changes in the colours and patterns. Clogs are worn by both sexes for everyday wear and work. In Marken they are varnished black with a coloured pattern and bear the wearer's initials. At one time in Scheveningen the clogs were sandpaper-white, whilst in other areas they were painted, decorated and carved. It was a custom for young men to present clogs which they had carved and decorated to their fiancées. For Sundays, clogs are exchanged for black shoes with silver buckles.

Plate 7 illustrates costumes from the fishing village of Volendam in the north. The woman wears a costume for Sunday wear, shown by the black apron with the decorated floral band at the top; on weekdays the aprons are striped. This costume consists of a 'tight wrap', made in the same material as the floral apron band; over this a tight fitting over-bodice or jacket with a braided square neckline is worn. Volendam women wear short hair which they tuck into a little black cap, on top of which is placed the lace winged cap. For mourning the 'tight wrap', apron band and beads would be black.

The man wears the black, baggy seaman's trousers, fastened in the front with silver buttons; at the back they are tied with a green cord, or black for mourning. The shirt collar is embroidered in black cross stitch and fastened with two gold studs. Over this a striped waistcoat and black jacket are worn; on Sundays another jacket with long sleeves is worn. The woollen scarf tucks into the striped waistcoat. In his fisherman's cap he wears three green ribbons at the back; one would indicate that he was engaged, but three mean that he is married.

FRANCE

The Frenchman is very much an individualist, possibly as a result of his mixed racial background, and this individuality is shown by the numerous costumes to be found throughout France. These are neat and precise; bodices, blouses and skirts are simple and show a clear-cut line. The skirts are not voluminous or pleated, although they allow plenty of room for movement. In many regions lace is made and here it is used for decorative purposes in the costumes. A main feature of French costumes are the hats and head-dresses, of which there are hundreds of different styles—One region can have a great deal of variation. Formerly sabots, or wooden clogs, were worn but now these are often replaced by an ordinary firm shoe. The most popular materials used are silks, velvet, wool, linen or striped or plain cotton.

BRITTANY

This is a region very different from the rest of the country as it is Celtic in origin. There are many interesting and unique festivals, some of them connected with the sea, and these are occasions when costumes are displayed. In some villages on Sundays the costumes are still worn to church.

One of the most attractive women's costumes is from Pont Aven, and is illustrated in Plate 9. It is worn at weddings, at one of the local 'Pardons' and on Sundays. The bodice is trimmed with velvet, braid and lace with a lace 'modesty vest' worn across the front opening. A large goffered collar is made of fine linen or muslin and is edged with lace; a special goffering iron is used to make the material fluted and stiff. The full skirt of satin or silk has a deep border of embroidered velvet, the embroidery being first done on tulle and then appliquéd on to the material. The head-dress or coif is made of stiffened lace and the two wings are fixed on to a little cap covered with blue ribbon. The ribbon is knotted into a bow to secure the ends of the lace. The old style of bibbed apron can be either white or blue and the dress either black or blue, with only a minimum amount of embroidery. There are several variations of this costume; the apron can be white and worn without the bib, the skirt can be plainer and have less decoration, the coif is in a different style according to the village of origin, but they all have the attractive lace collar.

The costume from Finisterre is interesting: the black bodice has a simple round neckline and long wide sleeves, all of which are covered with a fine silk braid in gold or deep orange. The patterns executed on the bodice and sleeves are extremely old and the circular designs reflect their Celtic origin. The skirt is black and a large white brocade or embroidered satin apron is worn over it. The coif is like a chimney pot made of stiffened lace. Black leather shoes have now replaced sabots.

For many years the men in Brittany wore full, baggy, white linen trousers called 'Bragou Braz'. These full trousers were fitted into long gaiters and are not unlike those worn in Holland and Sardinia. However, they have now been replaced by the more fashionable long trouser in dark blue, black or finely striped black and white. Over a white

37

shirt, a sleeved waistcoat is worn with a round neck, fastened with two rows of silver buttons. This waistcoat is made in two colours, a dark blue or black velvet upper section and a lighter blue in plain cloth for the remainder. Over this a black sleeveless jacket or chupen edged with embroidery is worn. In Finisterre the waistcoat is sleeveless and covered completely in deep orange braiding or in stripes of orange and gold; a black, long-sleeved jacket is worn over the waistcoat in this region. In Pont Aven the jacket is embroidered round the neck. Plate 9 shows a man from Quimper; his waistcoat is decorated with gold braid in a Celtic design of curling leaves. Men wear black felt hats with round crowns and brims with a rolling edge. A velvet ribbon is caught at the back with a silver buckle. At one time hand carved and decorated sabots were worn with the Bragou Braz but now ordinary black shoes are the custom.

NORMANDY

An outstanding feature of the costumes in Normandy is the very tall head-dress called Bourgoins. Made of starched muslin, fine linen and lace it is not unlike the Hennin which was popular in the fifteenth century. The head-dresses are made on a cone-shaped foundation and, although tall, are light in weight. In Calais the head-dress is pleated and starched and forms a halo round the face; it is worn with a high-necked, long-sleeved dress in royal blue, green or deep purple over which is a large black silk apron. The dress has a little stand-up collar, edged with white and fastened with a gold or silver brooch. White, pink or floral patterned shawls with fringed edges are tucked into the rather high waistband of the aprons. White gloves or black lace mittens give the costume a nineteenth century appearance. White or coloured stockings are worn with black shoes.

The men wear white or checked trousers with a blue smock and a red or white handkerchief tied round the neck. This is a basic costume found in many regions of France. In Calais the smock is shorter and a modern sailor's cap has replaced the small stocking cap formerly worn. Black shoes have again replaced sabots.

ALSACE

The traditions and costumes of Alsace have been influenced by both France and Germany.

The women wear black sleeveless velvet bodices laced up the front over white short sleeved blouses with a high frilled neckline. A red bow ties the gathers at the neck and sleeves. The skirt is red with two or three bands of black velvet ribbon round the hem. Aprons are of black silk and can be plain, embroidered with flowers on the lower edge or have an overall floral pattern on a black background. The most striking feature of the costume is the head-dress, which has a large silk bow fastened on to a little cap. The colour of the bow denotes the religion of the wearer: if black, Protestant, if red, Catholic. The colours of the skirts also denote religious faiths, red for Catholics, green for Protestants and mauve for Jewish people. Nowadays this colour pattern is not always strictly observed; for example, a black bow is often worn with a red skirt. A plain black shawl, or one with a floral design on a dark background, is occasionally worn draped across the shoulders. Stockings are white and shoes black with silver buckles.

Black trousers are worn by the men with red or pink brocade sleeveless waistcoats and a white shirt fastened at the neck with a black bow. A short black jacket is fastened with two rows of gold buttons. A black, flat crowned hat with a flat brim and black shoes are worn.

CHAMPAGNE

As in other regions, costumes are fairly simple, the main feature being the head-dress: an attractive one is made of two layers of gathered lace shaped into a halo, similar in style to those in Normandy, although smaller. Two pieces of ribbon are threaded through the lace and stand upright in the front. The long sleeved bodice and dress are of the same material—silk or cotton; colours of skirts tend to be dark, such as dark blue or dark orange. The aprons are of floral patterns on a white background. A white cotton fichu or shawl is draped round the shoulders and tucked into the waistband; it is also sometimes made of the same material as the dress. Sabots are worn for working, but are replaced by black leather shoes with silver buckles for Sundays, worn with white stockings.

The men wear a blue cotton apron and bib over brown trousers, and a white long-sleeved shirt fastened at the neck with a black bow tie. A black felt hat or peaked cap and sabots are also worn.

BURGUNDY

There is a wide range of costumes in this region with many unusual hats, and colours reflect the vines, grapes and wine.

A simple, but attractive, costume is worn by those working in the vineyards. This consists of a gathered skirt of striped cotton with pink, green or blue stripes on a white background. A silk or cotton apron in a darker shade is worn over the skirt; this may be of dark green with a green stripe, or burgundy with a pink stripe. A black, sleeveless, low-cut bodice, laced in front, is worn over a white V- or round-necked blouse with three-quarter length full sleeves. A fringed shawl of the same material and colour as the apron is draped round the shoulders and tucked into the top of the bodice. White cotton sun bonnets are worn and white stockings with low heeled black shoes replace the former heavy sabots.

Men wear black trousers with a deep burgundy sash and a brocaded waistcoat in yellow or gold. This waistcoat has lapels and a black back and black sleeves or, alternatively, a white back and sleeves. White shirts are worn with a burgundy bow tie. This costume can vary, the trousers can be striped and an apron worn over them. A peaked cap, as in Champagne, or a dark blue smock with a red scarf tied at the neck, may also be worn. Popular wooden sabots complete the costume.

PROVENCE

Provence is often described as 'the kingdom of the sun', and the climate has given a special quality and elegance to the costumes of the women, reflected in the colours and materials used. In Haute Provence the gathered skirts are of flowered cotton in pastel shades. The long-sleeved bodice can be either black or white and a fichu or shawl is draped across the shoulders and fastened at the waistband in the front. The apron is gathered into a small pointed basque and can be either black or white. In Basse Provence the skirt is sometimes in two stripes which have a combination of blue/red or yellow/white. A full sleeved blouse is worn and the apron and fichu are white. Attractive little white bonnets, which vary according to the area, are worn: they can be tied under the chin, crossed under the chin and tied at the top of the head or the ends just left loose.

The most elegant costume comes from Arles. Plate 8 shows a little girl dressed in this costume, which evolved in the middle of the nineteenth century and is known as the Mireille. Women wear their skirts long. The skirt, which may be made in a variety of colours, and bodice are of silk and the fichu is of lace or fine cotton edged with lace. The little white cap, of ribbon or lace, is known as a 'cravate' and is worn with a special hair style: the hair is parted down the middle and the two side pieces drawn back and combined with the back hair, forming a bun on the top of the head. A comb holds it in place and the long, white triangular cotton 'cravate' is tied round the bun with the ends forming a little bow in the front. Small children, not having so much hair, pin on the cravate in imitation of the adult style. White stockings and lightweight black shoes complete the costume.

The costume for the men is very simple; white trousers and shirts, a wide coloured sash with the ends tucked in and a dark patterned, sleeveless waistcoat. A red or blue beret or black felt hat is worn. The man in Plate 8 is dressed in a costume from Basse-Provence. Over the shirt of fine white cotton he wears a waistcoat of floral patterned velvet or silk brocade. The back is made of silk in a plain contrasting colour and is gathered into a half belt and buckle. The trousers can be pale beige, brown or white in colour and made either in velvet or cotton. A red, blue or black sash is tied round the waist. The black hat has a dent in the crown and is known as the Frivole. Black leather, lightweight shoes, sandals or rope soled espadrilles are worn.

BELGIUM

The costumes worn in Belgium are often very simple, both in style and design, and owe much to French, German and Dutch influence. The colours tend to be darker in the Flemish regions and brighter in the Walloon area.

Plate 10 shows the costume worn by Flemish girls. The full skirts are striped, usually dark blue or brown, and a frill is added to the hem or several lines of seams, which makes the bottom of the skirt stand out. The bodice is plain in colour, made either of cloth or silk, and fastens up to the neck; sleeves are long. Another touch of colour is added by the wearing of a Paisley shawl. These shawls became very popular in the nineteenth century when Scottish weavers developed the patterns found on material from Kashmir; the curved designs are based on the Indian mango shape. The bonnet is made of the white lace for which this region is famous; it either has ear flaps or two long streamers which hang down the back.

The Walloon girls also wear full skirts, with stripes ranging from a rather sober combination of greys, black and browns, to much brighter colours, but no frills are added. The bodice is cut as in the Flemish costume, but is of a brighter colour: the Paisley shawl is also worn. The Walloon girls wear an apron which can be either large with horizontal stripes, or small and of a plain colour. At Stavelot a poke bonnet of yellow straw is worn, called a 'chapeau à bavolet'. It is decorated with check ribbons and a white frill across the back, which protects the neck.

The men in both regions wear a blue linen smock, similar to that found in neighbouring countries. In Flanders it is very full (see Plate 10) and in the Walloon it is pleated, with a yoke. A shirt, fastened at the neck with coloured ribbons, is worn underneath, or the smock can be buttoned right up and then a red spotted handkerchief is worn. Dark trousers and a black or dark blue peaked cap complete the costume. Sabots used to be worn, but these have now been replaced by shoes; sometimes the girls wear leather bootees.

The costumes illustrated in Plate 10 are, in fact, now only worn by folk groups, although in some of the country areas the smock can still be seen.

GERMAN DEMOCRATIC REPUBLIC

The costumes of the German Democratic Republic are very varied and reflect the styles of neighbouring countries.

In the north the costumes have much in common with those of north Germany, Denmark and Sweden. The Baltic and Scandinavian areas are important for sheep rearing and consequently wool was used for costumes; the dyes were blue, red, green and yellow. Women favour red pleated skirts with a band of blue above the hem. A dark blue, long sleeved jacket is worn or, alternatively, a red and green skirt with a dark green jacket; the blouse worn underneath has a white frilled collar which shows above the high neckline. A short cape is draped and fastened round the shoulders in many of the northern districts exposed to the Baltic climate.

Plain coloured or perpendicular-striped aprons are worn and red stockings are very popular, for weddings the stockings are red and yellow. Green ribbons tied in bows beneath the knees act as garters. A little blue bonnet with a bow at the back, similar to the Danish headdress, is worn over a white under-cap. Older women wear a dark blue or black bonnet.

In the Mecklenburg lake district, a region halfway between the Baltic and Berlin, the women wear longer skirts and darker colours. A brown, long sleeved jacket is worn with a black skirt and the cape is replaced by a green shawl which is crossed over and tied at the back. Away from the Baltic winds the hats become more frivolous and a little straw hat is tied on with black ribbons with a black drape down the back.

Further south and west of Berlin, the styles change and are more influenced by city fashions. High necked, sleeveless black velvet bodices are worn over white long-sleeved blouses with frilled collars. The frills vary in size and can be quite large. Sometimes the bodice is patterned with flowers. The skirts can be striped in red or green, or pleated in red with a black border. Large black aprons are worn and the stockings are white. Little red bonnets with ribbons falling down the back tie on over a white lace under-cap.

Plate 11 shows two of the regional costumes. The woman on the left comes from Spreewald in the south-east, a picturesque forested region well known for its many costumes, traditional dialects and customs. A feature of this costume is the large padded head-dress called a 'lapa'. This is made from one large square silk or cotton scarf and two smaller ones, each embroidered and edged with lace, which are folded and pinned on to a stiffened base. The lapa can be in white or any pastel shade with a matching or contrasting shawl and apron.

The apron is made of white cotton, but often a fine plain or patterned voile is used. Skirts vary in colour and can be in black velvet to match the bodice, in red with a band of black or decorated with a band of floral taffeta edged with lace. There has been much competition between the women of this region which has resulted in many variations and the development of very elaborate head-dresses.

The woman on the right of Plate 11 wears a costume from the old region of Brandenburg which blends the styles of neighbouring countries, but which has an individuality of its own. The blue apron has braces which fasten on to the band at the back, showing a Bavarian influence. The pleated skirt and frilled blouse are similar to those worn in Bohemia (now Czechoslovakia). The dark blue sleeveless bodice has a high round neck, a style found in several costumes of the G.D.R. and Germany. The hat is made of felt and the head scarf is of black silk.

In the Harz mountains, full black skirts are covered by long white

43

aprons embroidered in yellow and tied at the waist with a yellow ribbon. A long sleeved black bodice is worn with or without a coloured shawl which has the ends tucked into the waist. Several rows of gold necklaces brighten the black bodice. A little cap with long black ribbons down the back or tied into a bow, similar to that worn in Alsace, is worn. White stockings and black low heeled shoes, the type of footwear found in most regions, are worn.

Men's costumes are based on the frock coat which was popular in the nineteenth century. In the Baltic region they are blue with a red lining and have lapels and a collar. The buttons are silver and underneath the coat a blue waistcoat is worn. Breeches are of yellow buckskin or made of wool, and the black leather boots are knee length. A white collar is worn with a black silk bow. A broad brimmed felt hat has ribbons at the back, but top hats, decorated with flowers and green ribbons, are worn at weddings.

In Mecklenburg the blue coat is cut without lapels and the breeches are replaced by yellow trousers worn with purple stockings and black shoes. A high necked green woollen waistcoat is fastened with a double row of buttons. A black scarf is tied at the neck and a black top hat is worn.

In the Berlin area the costume consists of a red lined, blue coat without lapels, yellow breeches, high boots and a blue waistcoat with a double row of buttons. A black scarf is again tied round the neck, and the black top hat has a buckle in front.

In the Harz region, a countryman would wear black breeches tucked into gaiters. The blue frock-coat is lined with red and has brass buttons or silver for Sundays; the high, patterned waistcoat is similar to that of other areas. Black shoes are worn.

WEST GERMANY

The country we now know as West Germany was formerly a patchwork of kingdoms, electoral principalities, grand duchies and duchies. Thus it is only natural that strong individual traits should have developed, giving rise to the great range of costumes found in West Germany today.

For the purpose of describing costume West Germany can be roughly divided into north and south by using the old Roman frontier based on the rivers Main and Rhine.

The relaxed way of life of the southern Germans and Rhinelanders is shown in their costumes and the use of colours, as well as their dancing; brighter colours are used for skirts, bodices and aprons, with red and yellow strongly featured. The costumes of the people in the north tend to be more sober in colouring and they favour such colours as black, blues, greens and purples.

The Germans have a great love of music and a fondness for carnivals, festivals, folk dancing and other folklore occasions for wearing costumes. Peasants from the Ries plains, the inhabitants of the Black Forest and of Bavaria still wear their native costumes when they come into the towns on market days or for the many festivals.

Women's costumes throughout the country show numerous ways of wearing bodice, blouses, skirts and aprons. The bodice, known as a 'Laibli' or 'Leibli', can be sleeveless and fastened down the front, the neck edge, armholes and front fastenings being decorated with braid, velvet or pleated ribbons; the bodice can be quite plain or embroidered with a pattern of flowers. In some areas sleeves, made of the same material, are attached to the bodice and the cuffs, neckline and front fastening are bound with velvet of a deeper shade. A very attractive bodice in black velvet and edged with braid and pearl buttons comes from the Black Forest. A blue or green bodice edged with red braid is another colourful variation and is found in the south. In the region bordering Switzerland bodices are laced across with coloured ribbons, leaving a wide gap in which a panel of plain or embroidered velvet is worn, and underneath this is a blouse.

Many picturesque costumes are found in the Black Forest region and they vary from village to village. A feature of the costumes is a decorative yoke called a halsmantel or halsband. This was originally separate, fitted over the bodice and kept in place by four ribbons which pass from the corners and tie in bows under each arm. The halsmantel can be embroidered, edged with a trimming or have a gathered frill. It varies considerably according to district and village and sometimes it has a little stand-up collar or a frilled band around the neck. Now, the halsmantel is often made as part of the costume.

Skirts are full, sometimes pleated and sometimes made of striped material, but mostly they are in plain colours. Many petticoats are worn, allowing for freedom of movement when performing some of the vigorous turning and couple dances.

The woman in Plate 13 is dressed in a costume from Bavaria; the

45

bodice is tied across the front with a cord of silver chain, passing round silver hooks. The fringed shawl is of wool or silk and the beads fasten at the neck with a gold or silver clasp. Posies are worn at the tops of bodices and a flower is fixed into the gold cord of the hat; an eagle's feather sometimes replaces the flower. Several white petticoats are worn under the red woollen dress and the stockings are knitted in a ribbed pattern. There are variations of this costume, the skirt being black and the apron can have a floral pattern.

Aprons are worn in most regions, but tend to be plain in the north and flowered, braided or embroidered in the south. German costumes are not embroidered a great deal; embroidery is found on bodices, hems of aprons, and front panels and yokes, although not in great profusion. The flowers embroidered on the bodice worn by the woman in Plate 12 are those found in the Schwarzwald region. Her skirt is of silk taffeta.

One of the important features of German costume is the hat, each region and village having a different style. In the area near Alsace, a large bow type of head-dress is worn, similar to those worn across the border. If a girl is unmarried, she wears a plait down her back, but married women tuck their hair into little black caps worn underneath the bow. There are many flat straw hats, sometimes yellow or lacquered white, and in the Black Forest these are decorated with woollen pom poms, red for the unmarried girl, black for denoting marriage (see Plate 12). The number of pom poms varies according to the area: there can be seven large ones attached to the crown or eleven small ones arranged in the shape of a cross. Another hat has four little groups of pom poms clustered to the sides of the crown. A married woman usually wears a black cap underneath the straw hat.

There are also tall hats, little hats made from ribbons, hats with eye veils, hats decorated with ribbons on the crown, hats denoting religious denomination and the very lovely bridal crowns or Schappel, made of flowers, ribbons, beads, pearls and glass.

The young girls wear their hair in plaits or plaited and bound round the head and, on special occasions, plaited with ribbons. Stockings are white and the shoes usually black.

The little girl in Plate 12 wears a costume from the Schwalm valley in Hesse, central Germany. A padded roll is tied round the waist and over this go numerous petticoats before the final woollen skirt and apron, giving a high waistline effect. The first petticoat is a narrow one to prevent the legs being shown during some of the boisterous dances. The stockings are tied under the knees with red garter ribbons. Her hair is worn up and a tiny head-dress made of ribbons on a round stiffened base is fixed on top of the head.

The men's costumes are similar in style to those found in other Teutonic countries: knee breeches, waistcoats, jackets, shirts and hats with variations according to region.

The knee breeches are often black or of a dark colour, with embroidery on the front flaps and on the sides. The breeches in the north tend to be plainer and those in the south a little more decorative. In Bavaria the breeches are replaced by leather shorts common to both Germany and Austria. Plate 13 shows a gentleman from Bavaria dressed in the short leather 'lederhosen' which are decorated with oak leaves. Broad, decorated braces with a cross-band showing above the waistcoat hold up the trousers.

Waistcoats are worn in most regions but vary considerably in design. They can be double breasted, fastening up to the neck by means of two rows of gold buttons: sometimes the upper part is turned back to form lapels and revealing the shirt underneath which is worn with a knotted scarf. A single breasted V-neck waistcoat is sometimes worn and in some villages along the Rhine a type of sleeveless vest or pullover is very popular. This garment, scarlet in colour, has a round neck decorated with black velvet braid. Scarlet waistcoats, vests and shirts look very striking when worn with the black breeches, jackets or coats.

The wearing of scarlet denotes that the wearer is married: white is worn only by bachelors. In the south, gaily decorated braces are found and again marital status is denoted by the embroidery: if executed in white then the wearer is married, if in red then the wearer is still single. Also, a married man turns the brim of his hat up and the unmarried has his brim down.

Long-sleeved jackets reaching to the waist or hips and decorated with one or two rows of buttons are worn over the many kinds of waistcoats. These jackets can be black, brown, red or blue and are often lined with a contrasting colour. The buttons can be of silver, shaped like a coin or, alternatively, carry a design. In the north the jackets reaching to below waist level are cut straight to the neck with a round edge or slight stand-up collar. In Bavaria the jackets are of a grey, thick showerproof cloth called Loden, and the lapels, cuffs and edges are bound in green and the buttons made of horn. Three buttons are on either side of the jacket, with one on each of the lapels. Long knee-length coats replace the jackets in some areas.

In the Schalm valley and on the Ries plain, a large blue smock is worn which has white braid on the shoulders and around the neck. This garment has its counterpart in France and Switzerland and is very reminiscent of the basic European tunic.

White shirts are worn in most areas with flat or stand-up collars, together with red or black bows or knotted ties.

Black top hats with a green head-band fastened in the front with a buckle are found in many areas. Black, round beaver hats with varying sized brims curling inwards are also popular and in the north a black tricorne is worn. In Bavaria green felt hats, decorated with a chamois plume, are worn. At one time woodmen working in the forests used to wear black varnished straw hats with square crowns, their hat denoting their craft.

White or black socks worn with silver buckled black shoes are the most usual footwear. In Bavaria (see Plate 13) old style knitted socks without feet may be worn; these were evolved as heavy shoes continually wore holes in the toes and heels of the socks. If leather breeches are worn they are tucked into white ribbed knitted stockings.

AUSTRIA

When Austria lost her empire in 1918 a strong nationalist feeling developed in the country with a revival of peasant costumes and dances, and with the coming of the Salzburg Music Festival the dirndl dress was created. This is now the most popular costume. Basically it is a full skirt, a bodice of either wool, cotton or velvet which is laced or buttoned up with silver buttons. A white short or long sleeved blouse is worn under the bodice. On weekdays plain or coloured cotton aprons cover the skirts, but on Sundays silk aprons are worn. The dirndl differs in colour, materials and design, and can be simple or elaborate. There are regional variations in the bodice neckline. This costume is used by folk dancers in preference to the more elaborate regional dresses. Plate 14 illustrates the basic dirndl dress; this is a simple, everyday one made of cotton.

Men have a costume which is also very popular and is worn by young and old alike. There are two styles, the lederhosen—chamois leather shorts or breeches—and the long woollen suits. Lederhosen are probably the most practical form of trousers in existence, and are thought to have been originated by the Celts. Grey or black in colour they are worn with embroidered braces and ornamental belts. The short style are usually worn for dancing or by young boys. A white open-necked shirt with rolled-up sleeves is worn, occasionally with a tie. White stockings and black shoes complete the costume.

For more formal wear coats, jackets and trousers are made from a thick woollen felt-like material called loden, in grey, green or brown. It is very warm and weatherproof.

Skirts in all of the regions are full and often pleated. In Vorarlberg young girls wear a white pleated skirt gathered into a small red yoke or bodice cut in high Empire style. A black belt gathers the pleats in at the waist. Married women wear similar skirts, but in black with the yoke embroidered in gold. In the Tyrol, skirts are usually red or black and gathered rather than pleated. In the state of Burgenland skirts are white with a slight pattern, similar to those worn in Hungary. The skirts worn in Carinthia, the most southern state, are all accordion pleated; black and brown are the most popular colours, the hems being edged with a green or coloured border. Embroidered belts which have bunches of coloured ribbons hanging from the waist are worn.

Many of the Austrian dances are couple dances which involve a great number of turns, so several white cotton petticoats are worn under the skirts. In the Tyrol red and green bodices are worn over white blouses and in the east the bodices are dark and the blouses are long-sleeved. In Upper Austria at Innviertel a tight-fitting plum coloured jacket with a basque replaces the bodice. The full skirt is in the same colour and a gold shawl is draped over the shoulders.

Some of the regional costumes have long-sleeved bodices and skirts made in the same material. Those from the Ziller valley are in black with a square neckline and gathered sleeves. In the Lower Inn Valley the dress is in maroon and in Wachau, Lower Austria, it is made in gold or blue brocade with a draped neckline. Blue, green, gold and orange aprons are popular, and for Sunday wear they are often made in silk or brocade.

There are many different hats: in Salzburg little round felt boaters have a gold cord round the crown with two tassels. The women of Innviertel wear a strange gold hat which fans out like a bird's tail. In Wachau the hat opens out like a halo. In Vorarlberg the children wear a golden crown tied on with black ribbons and the women wear fur hats. When the French Army was retreating in 1809, many of Napoleon's men threw away their caps and these were retrieved by village girls, who wore them to mock the former victors and thus a new fashion was created. In the Tyrol (see Plate 14) women wear felt hats lined with red.

White, blue, red and green stockings knitted in a rib or another pattern, are worn with silver buckled black shoes laced with red ribbons. In Burgenland the stockings and ankle boots are black. In this region the men wear breeches made of wool or leather, in black, brown or grey. These leather breeches will often have a design worked on the wide seams or the front opening. Red waistcoats are very popular and are fastened with either a single or double row of silver, brass or horn buttons. In the Tyrol the waistcoats are made with round necks and have side fastenings. Decorated broad leather belts and braces are worn over these waistcoats. In the mountain regions the colder weather demands thick breeches with waistcoats and jackets made from loden material. Plate 14 illustrates a man dressed for climbing in the Tyrol.

Jackets vary in colour and can be blue, brown, green or grey. In Styria the grey jacket is short with a green collar, cuffs and lapels. In Upper Austria the jacket reaches to below the hips and is similarly decorated. In the Salzburg region the jacket is green and reaches to the hips. On most of the jackets the buttons are of silver or horn.

The Tyrol is an area which provides much of the wool, leather, horn and silver used in the making of costumes. At one time it was reputed that the miners were so rich that the nails in their boots were made of silver.

White shirts are worn with most costumes and have red or black knotted ties or bows. Hats are very popular and range from broad alpine felt hats to fur and the felt caps of Burgenland. In the Tyrol there is an arrangement of plumes from the feathers of the black mountain cock, the eagle and other wild birds. The bunches of feathers are fixed into the hat bands and are known as 'scheibenbart'.

In the Salzburg region black or green hats have the traditional 'gamsbart', which is a chamois brush. Gold cord and two tassels decorate some black felt hats and complement those worn by the women. A posy of flowers is often fixed into the hat band.

White, blue or green knitted stockings are worn with black shoes, either laced or with silver buckles.

SWITZERLAND

Swiss costumes show the influence of neighbouring countries as well as having a definite style of their own. In the seventeenth and eighteenth centuries Switzerland was renowned for her lovely silks, ribbons, braids and embroideries and these materials were incorporated by the peasants into their costumes. Designs and embroidery are very colourful, reflecting the wild flowers of the country. The French influence is shown in the pastel shades used in dress and aprons. Striped or floral print bodices and skirts are worn with plain coloured aprons or a dark dress is worn with an apron of pastel stripes. Small lace fichus or fringed shawls are draped or tucked into the top of the bodice. Trim little caps or bonnets, attractive flat yellow straw hats or winged black lace hats made on wire frames are all very popular in the west. Black lace mittens extending to the elbows are worn when the bodice or blouse sleeves are short. The costumes are very neat and this quality is reflected in the dance steps and music of the western area.

The woman illustrated in Plate 15 wears a costume from Emmental and Plateau in the canton of Berne. The bodice, of black velvet, is worn over a white blouse which has very fine pleats in the front. The yoke which was once separate is now part of the costume, but the silver clips and chains which hold it in place still remain. The bodice is laced with a silver chain or white cord wound round silver hooks. The apron is of taffeta and the head-dress is made of horsehair or net gathered on to a little cap. A similar costume from the same region has a pale blue cotton skirt, a white or pale grey apron, and yellow yoke and front bodice edged with black braid. The lacing is black, but the sides and back of the bodice are red. As this is a working costume there are no lace mittens. Hair is worn in two pigtails tied with long black ribbons and there is a little flat straw hat.

The costumes from the German speaking districts are less simple than the western style: colours are darker, for example browns, deeper shades of blue, black relieved by white, pink, green, blue or striped aprons. The bodices are a feature of this region and bear a similarity to those worn in the Black Forest. A costume from Berne has a bodice with red back and sides, and a yellow centre panel over which black ribbon is laced around silver buttons. The yoke, which stems from the German halsmantel, is edged with black velvet. In some of the costumes the halsmantel or collerette is still worn, in others it has been incorporated into the bodice. In Germany the halsmantel is tied on with ribbons: in Switzerland, silver chains with filigree rosette attachments are clipped on to the front and back of the bodice. This decoration is found on many Swiss costumes.

Little flat straw hats, little black hats which sit on the back of the head, tied on with ribbons, and little hats like halos are very popular. Long- or short-sleeved blouses are usual.

The Italian love of colours is shown in the costumes in the southern region. A red bodice laced over a white panel and worn with a white blouse, a green skirt, a violet apron patterned with flowers on the border and a blue shawl edged with coloured bands tucked into the bodice is an example. Brightly coloured head scarves, knotted at the back, are preferred to hats.

On the Austrian border and in the Romansch-speaking region, skirts are accordion pleated in red, blue, green, yellow and black. Bodices tend to be more elaborate: one from the Haute-Engadine in the Canton Grisons has a red, long-sleeved bodice with a black velvet panel, a little black cape and also a black apron, all embroidered with flowers using gold thread. A white frilled collar, amber beads and a tiny skull cap complete this costume.

In Appenzell, tight fitting black bodices are worn with brightly coloured skirts and, for festive occasions, a long-sleeved jacket with a spectacular collar of white pleated lace edged with black is added. It is here that the lovely head-dress made like two butterfly wings in black tulle, with a pleated white inset, is worn. White stockings worn with silver buckled black shoes are most common, but occasionally red or mauve stockings are worn.

The men in several of the cantons wear a hip length, long-sleeved smock in black or blue, worn over long black trousers and a white shirt. The neck opening has a wide V-line with borders of floral embroidery repeated on the shoulders and cuffs. The white shirt is fastened at the neck with a knotted ribbon with pom poms at the ends. The working smock is plain white, fastened at the neck and with a hood for protection against the sun. This was the basic outdoor costume but, like the English smock, it has now gone out of fashion.

In Gruyère and the Oberland the herdsmen wear blue or black jackets with short sleeves: those from Gruyère are blue and have embroidered edelweiss on the lapels and a design down the edge.

The men in this area carry a black embroidered shoulder bag holding salt for the cows to lick. Their white collared shirts have specially pleated sleeves in an horizontal design. The shirt is buttoned at the neck and no tie is worn. In Oberland the sleeves are plain and a little black bow tie is worn.

Skull caps of leather, felt or velvet, which are decorated with tassels are worn but black felt hats are worn with the smocks. The shoes can either be laced or have silver buckles.

Plate 15 illustrates the traditional costume worn by a herdsman in the Appenzell and Toggenbourg regions. The yellow breeches are made of soft leather and across the left hip a handkerchief is tied. The handkerchiefs are decorated with patterns of the herd, the names of the animals or proverbs of the area. Silver chains with old coins at the end hang from the waist. The red woollen jacket is edged with braid and the square silver buttons are either plain or have filigree designs. On the lapel is embroidered a sun, a star or a flower. The leather braces have a cross section decorated with a line of cows. The same motif is used in embroidery on the edge of the shirt and patterned on the collar brooch and the buckles of the shoes. In his right ear he wears a little ring with a tiny silver ladle attached. The black felt hat is decorated with flowers and ribbons.

ITALY

Many existing Italian costumes, embroidery, designs, patterns of materials and dances stem from the Renaissance period. Before the unification of Italy under Victor Emmanuel, the various states had developed their own characteristics, customs and costumes and, consequently, there is today a great variation in the numerous costumes to be found.

In the north, the predominant colours are blue, green, purple and black; in the south, reds, greens and maroon colours are preferred and near to the sea there is a predilection for blue. Red is favoured by brides and married women. Heavy materials, such as damask, heavy taffeta and wool, are used for the skirts.

Blouses are made of linen or cotton, bodices and jackets of velvet and aprons of lace, silk, cotton, linen or velvet. Necklaces of coral, chains of silver or gold and filigree brooches are worn extensively.

In the north, many costumes bear a strong resemblance to those of the Tyrol. Skirts are full and covered by large aprons; plum red or dark blue aprons are worn over black or plum red skirts. Bodices are very popular in Italy; in the north, they are sleeveless and made in red or green woollen material edged with a contrasting colour and laced up the front over a red panel. White blouses have full sleeves and a high frilled neckline with a black velvet cross-over ribbon pinned at the throat.

A costume worn by young girls at the Easter festival in Val d'Isarco in the Dolomites, has a full black skirt covered by a large white lace apron tied in the front with a pink ribbon. The red bodice is edged with green and laced over a contrasting panel. The blouse with its little stand-up collar has a frilled yoke (similar to the German halsband). In the Val d'Aosta the bodice is replaced by a long-sleeved black or blue velvet jacket with an inset panel embroidered in gold. Large brimmed, black felt hats are decorated with a green hat band and a silver buckle and these are worn in several regions. In Val d'Aosta, a bonnet type hat made of stiffened gold thread lace is worn. A similar hat is made in white lace, decorated with flowers and ribbons on the crown. Where a hat is not worn, the hair is sometimes dressed in a bun which is studded with silver pins. In Lombardy the pins are large and have filigree ends, giving a shimmering halo effect. Black leather shoes and white stockings are customary.

In central Italy in the regions of the Marches, Umbria, Latium, Abruzzi and Molise, there is great variety in costume. The skirts are long and made from homespun material in black or, for special occasions, in red. Large aprons covering the skirts are made in blue, brown or white cotton or, alternatively, in a white floral brocade. The blouse is often made in the same material as the skirt and those from Scanno, Abruzzi, have a large full sleeve gathered into deep cuffs.

The most usual form of head-dress seen in central and southern areas is the 'tovaglia'. Designed to protect the back of the neck and the head from the sun, it can be worn in many different ways. It is made from linen which is starched and folded to form a type of hat. In parts of the Marches it is folded into three, facing the back of the head, and is secured with pins. In Abruzzi, a lace or white scarf is first draped over the head and the material then folded across the top. In Latium, the edge of the white material is scalloped and embroidered in white, the flat upper front section being rolled under. The tovaglia are usually white, but if two are worn then the top one is heavily embroidered or coloured. The material when folded is kept in place by long pins with decorated ends. A silver pin is worn by young girls and a gold pin by a bride or married women. In Letino and Gallo Matese in the Campania, the women's head-dress is called the 'mappelana'. If green in colour the wearer is unmarried and, if red, she is married: black denotes widowhood.

The woman's costume from Aviano in Plate 16 shows a blend of both the northern and central fashions.

The bodice is made of velvet or can be in a homespun wool like the skirt. These dresses are passed down from mother to daughter and several deep tucks may be found where the length has needed adjusting. The apron is in light wool or cotton and the blouse made of fine linen. Several petticoats would be worn and the stockings handknitted in cotton. The black rope-soled shoes are of velvet or felt and embroidered with silk or wool.

Towards the south skirts are pleated, black and red being the most popular colours. In Frosinore (Latium) two brightly coloured skirts are worn, the upper one being gathered round the hips and pinned under a dark apron, giving a pannier effect. A feature of this area is the oblong shaped, double fronted apron; these are sometimes plain or have a wide border of embroidery. An alternative is in brocade where one end of the apron is folded to form a short upper apron over the larger one.

An unusual bodice with separate sleeves is worn both in Abruzzi and Molise; in black velvet and cut low in front, it is worn over a long-sleeved white blouse. A black velvet sleeve is then pulled over the blouse leaving a gap of five or six inches between the top of the sleeve and the shoulder through which the blouse sleeve protrudes.

In Monteroduni (Molise) the sleeves and bodice are red velvet edged with silver braid; they are worn with a red pleated skirt and black apron. In some regions of Molise the bodice sleeve reaches only to above the elbow. Blouses are in white cotton and when worn with a short bodice sleeve, the full sleeve of the blouse is finely pleated horizontally. Shawls or fichus of lace or floral material are tucked into the top of the bodice.

The shoe characteristic of the central regions is the soft black leather ciocie; one of the earliest forms of footwear, it is similar to a ballet pump with cross lacing over the foot and is tied round the ankles and legs. White or black stockings are usual.

In the far south of Italy, in the regions of Puglie, Basilicata and Calabria, colours are more vivid and the skirts are fuller. Pleated skirts are still very popular, but the pleats are very tight and narrow at the waist and hips, opening into broader ones. The pleats are made by first dampening the material, pressing in the pleats and hanging the skirt up to dry. Under repeated processing, the pleats become practically permanent. In some areas of Calabria two pleated skirts are worn, both with a deep gold border. The upper skirt is folded back in the front and secured, or tucked under the arm.

In Taranto (Puglie) long-sleeved coloured jackets are worn with vividly coloured skirts. Jackets are tightly waisted and flounce over the hips. A triangular lace fichu partly covers the jacket front, reaching from the shoulder to a point at the waist. Dark blue jackets partner red skirts, light blue with yellow, pink with blue, or green with brown skirts, thus giving many colour combinations.

It is probable that at Taranto the famous dance, the Tarantella, originated and Plate 17 illustrates a boy and girl from Naples about to dance. The girl wears several petticoats under her blue silk skirt. Her high-cut black velvet bodice, which is partly hidden by the wide collar of the blouse is tied with a large silk bow. The white ribbed stockings are worn with light, flexible shoes necessary for the nimble footwork of this famous dance.

The boy has a gold brocade or velvet waistcoat and his red breeches fasten at the knees with silver or gold buttons. The fisherman's red hat is of a style found in most of the Mediterranean ports. Made of wool, it provides good protection in all weathers as it clings firmly to the head.

In Sorrento the dancers wear black or red velvet sleeveless bodices, cut low in the front and high at the back. White blouses have little puff sleeves and round the low and rather wide neckline is a large gathered frill. Skirts are made of a heavy red, green or black silk with a braided border or a design round the hem. The apron is of a very fine white lace which allows the colour of the skirt to show through. White stockings are worn with black lightweight shoes with a small heel.

Men's costumes are simpler. In the north, black leather breeches or shorts with the front flap and side seams piped in white are worn. A red waistcoat with a round, high neck is fastened up the front with white or metal buttons and this is worn under a red or black jacket edged with green. Broad green braces are worn over the waistcoat with a wide black decorated belt.

A white, long-sleeved shirt with a turned-down collar is fastened at the neck with a brooch, tie or bow. There is a black felt hat with a round flat brim and a black chin strap. Fastened on to the front of the hat with a cord and two tassels is a bunch of flowers, small feathers and two or four very long white tail feathers from a mountain bird.

With the shorts, black leather braces, similar to a wide bib, and decorated with an Alpine design of open leatherwork are worn over a black waistcoat and white shirt. A small, round, black, narrow brimmed Alpine hat with a red or black hat band with a tassel at the back is also worn. The white shirt has a small stand-up collar and is fastened at the neck. No tie is worn.

White stockings tied at the knees with black or red garters and black shoes go with both types of costume.

Away from the mountain regions, the men wear long black trousers, waistcoats of velvet or wool in a variety of colours and designs. These are single-breasted with a row of gold or plain buttons. A silk or cotton sash is tied around the waist and in the north the ends of the sash are tucked into the trousers. A white linen long-sleeved shirt, sometimes without a collar, is worn open at the neck.

A black or green felt hat is decorated with flowers in the summer or, with coloured woollen balls. In these regions the shoes are similar to those worn by the women. Plate 16 illustrates the man's costume from Aviano in the north.

Towards the central and southern areas the men's costume maintains a similar style. Black, dark green or brown breeches replace the long trousers and they are made of wool or velveteen. In some areas the breeches reach to just below the knees and are tight fitting, fastened at the knees with two or three buttons or a coloured garter tied in a bow. In Taranto, light brown breeches reach down to mid-calf and are loose in style. Waistcoats trimmed with gold buttons are made of silk, velvet or wool: they are frequently the same colour as the trousers. On the Neapolitan coast, waistcoats are blue, red or green and are worn with red or black breeches. The front and back of the waistcoat may be of contrasting colours. A wide sash in plain or striped material is tied at the waist, with the ends falling on the left side.

Shirts are made of white cotton or linen and have long sleeves. Round the collar or the neck is worn a knotted scarf and in the north this is usually of a floral design on a dark background: in the south they are red or some other vivid colour.

Hats have a flat or slightly raised crown with a small brim. In coastal areas the fisherman's red stocking cap is more popular.

ENGLAND

England is a country rich in folklore and traditions yet has little variety in her folk costumes.

Folk dancing, however, has always played an important part in the life of the people and English country dancing has influenced the dancing in other countries; for example, the dances of Canada and the U.S.A. developed from those brought over by the early English settlers.

The most well known costumes are those of the Morris dancers. Divided into two styles, Country and English Morris, there are many speculations on the derivation of the name 'Morris' but a general theory is that it betrays the Moorish influence introduced via the Spanish. It may have roots even further back in Africa and Asia stemming from Sufic traditions.

Morris dances were performed only by men at certain times of the year, in teams of six or eight with a Squire and Bagman in charge. These dances had ritualistic and magical meanings associated with the awakening of the earth. The dancers carried either sticks, swords or white handkerchiefs. The theme of animal worship is shown in one of the oldest of the Morris dances which comes from Abbotts Bromley in Staffordshire, where the dancers carry the antlers of deer: the Morris men of Abingdon carry the head of a bull as their emblem.

Plate 18 illustrates a Morris dancer. The costume changes from team to team; the slight variations depending upon the area they represent. Basically it consists of white trousers, shirt, a pad of bells around the calf of the leg and a decorated felt hat. On the rosette worn on the chest is the emblem of the team. The hat changes slightly with each team and can be made of either felt or straw. The be-ribboned and decorated hat shown in Plate 18 is made of straw and has red poppies as a sign of health, wheat as a sign of plenty while the blue cornflowers are a sign of single blessedness. The white handkerchiefs waved by the dancers symbolised the gathering and scattering of magic and energy over the ground and crops.

The sword dancing teams wear dark breeches, white shirts and sleeveless jackets, but no calf bells. The present costume has gradually evolved through fairly recent years, the dancers of the past performing in the dress of their period.

An unusual costume which has not altered is from Bacup, Lancashire, where the dancers black their faces, wear black jerseys, breeches and a short black and white skirt. Coconut shells are used to create a rhythm and a similar dance is found in Provence, France.

The dress for English country dancing is also fairly recent, though for many years peasant costumes dating from the eighteenth and nineteenth centuries were used for folk dance presentations. The girls wore laced-up bodices, blouses, skirts with a pannier effect, and bonnets or mob caps.

The men wore the old country smock, very similar in style to those found in France, Germany and other countries. A feature of the English smock was the embroidery on the yoke, shoulders and wrists, known as smocking. From the colour of the smock it was possible to tell the region of the wearer and from the embroidery on the collar or side panels, the occupation or trade of the wearer. At the yearly hiring at fairs, the farmers could read the symbols on the smocks of those waiting to be hired.

IRELAND

Throughout its troubled history a strong folklore has grown up in Ireland together with a wealth of folk traditions. The people were very poor, but had a great sense of enjoyment so that weddings and funerals were occasions for entertainments which would last for several days. They believed in sending the dead soul on its journey with merriment and there was plenty of dancing, accompanied by a piper or a fiddler, together with much singing.

Life for the Irish peasant was not easy and clothes were simple and functional. Many went bare-footed or wore primitive shoes made from animal skins and these were still being worn at the beginning of this century.

The climate is damp and both men and women wore woollen cloaks, known as brats. These garments had an attached hood to be pulled over the head on a cold day and the cloak would be fastened to the shoulder or chest by means of a Tara brooch, or tied under the chin with a black bow of corded ribbon. These cloaks were worn all over Ireland in the seventeenth century, by rich and poor alike, and may still be seen occasionally in parts of Cork. The wool was particularly thick and durable, being resistant to the weather. Black, red, blue and grey were the most popular colours, red particularly as the madder root, found in many parts of the country, was used as a dye. A mother would present her daughter with a new cloak on her wedding day and this would be kept for special occasions, the old one being worn for going to market.

The Irish were at one time expert metal workers and used intricate Celtic designs which are often reflected in their dances. Irish dancing is extremely popular and, as with Scottish dancing, is performed all over the world. The costumes that would be worn at a Feis were evolved fairly recently and were designed for the quick, neat footwork and leg action found in the choreography of Irish dancing.

The Irish couple in Plate 18 are wearing costumes used for dancing. These costumes were evolved to suit the growth and development of Irish dancing and incorporated certain features of rural dress. The traditional cloak has now become very short and is worn for decoration only. The shape of the dress is now established, but each school or team of dancers have their own variation and colour. Green is the most popular colour for both kilts and dresses as it reflects the green of Ireland as well as St. Patrick's emblem, the shamrock. The cloak worn by the girl has been adapted to a half drape and has an embroidered Celtic design. Both the cloak and the man's plaid are fastened on the shoulder by a Tara brooch. The shoes can be made from a hard or soft pliable leather, according to the type of dance being performed. The man's kilt can be either green or saffron.

SCOTLAND

Although closely linked geographically, Scotland and England have their own highly developed characteristics since the Gaelic speaking clansmen bore the surnames of their respective chiefs and later wore their colours or tartans.

The Scots, as in many other countries, had a tunic or shirt made from a coarse material and dyed the popular saffron colour, which had the added quality of being an insect repellent. In the extreme winter weather of the Highlands, a length of woollen material was wrapped round the body and worn both by men and women. This developed into the kilt and plaid and served two purposes, a warm outer garment by day and a blanket by night. The material was worn pleated round the lower part of the body and held by a belt and the remainder was draped over the shoulder, being pulled around the upper body according to need. By the mid eighteenth century the lower half had become a separate garment known as the feile beg or little kilt.

During the Stuart rising of 1745, in support of Prince Charles' claim to the throne, the English forbade the wearing of the kilt, together with the playing of bagpipes and other traditional highland customs, condemning them as too nationalistic. As a result of this, 'trews' were worn; these were a combination of stockings and breeches, cut in cloth and mostly favoured by the upper classes.

It is uncertain when tartans were first used, but there is mention of them in the sixteenth and seventeenth centuries. In the eighteenth century they became recognised and acknowledged as identification between the clans.

The kilt is still worn by both Highland regiments and as part of everyday dress. There are two distinct styles of Scottish dress: the everyday and social and the dress for Highland dancing. During the day the man wears a tweed jacket, usually lovat green, with his kilt, a white shirt and stockings to match the jacket, with thick brown brogue shoes.

The sporran is made of leather and is used as a purse and, in the past, also acted as a protection to the body. Women have no definite costume. For evening wear or festive occasions, the man wears the costume as illustrated in Plate 19 but the doublet or coatee is usually black. Black evening shoes or pumps would be worn with this costume. To match the man's finery at a Highland Ball, the woman would pin her tartan plaid to her evening dress. If the wife of a chieftain or colonel it is worn from the left shoulder, otherwise from the right side.

For Scottish country dancing, the man wears either the day or evening dress and the woman a short or long full-skirted dress and draped plaid.

For Highland dancing, which is usually performed at Highland Games and championships, the costume is as illustrated in Plate 19. The man's jacket is made of velvet or cloth and he can wear either the doublet or a coatee. The black leather dirk belt has a silver buckle and his sporran is in the pattern used for evening wear, made of fur which is usually sealskin, with a metal top.

The kilt illustrated is in the Buchanan tartan and the matching stockings have red flashes protruding from the tops. A skean dhu (or dagger) fits down the side of the stocking. On his head he wears a woollen Balmoral bonnet with a silver crest on the side. Alternatively this could be a Glengarry which resembles a forage cap. Black Highland pumps are laced across the instep and round the ankles. His white jabot is made of lace, but if he was wearing a coatee this would be replaced by a black bow tie.

The girl's costume shows the very fine pleating of the kilt at the back. Her tartan is Stewart Dress which is red and black on a white background. The jacket is in black velvet, the most popular colour for both men and women although alternative colours can be worn. The front of the jacket is fastened at the waist and shows a white lace-fronted blouse. The edge is trimmed with silver braid and has a row of five ornamental buttons on each side of the front and also on the sleeve vent. She wears a Balmoral type bonnet and her stockings match the tartan kilt. Women do not wear the skean dhu, sporran, belt, plaid flashes, Glengarry bonnets or bows. The black Highland pumps are similar to those of the man.

WALES

Although Wales is physically joined to England, the Welsh, like the Scots, have developed their own characteristics. The Welsh language is particularly musical and the country is renowned for its singing and choirs. Each year an Eisteddfod is held, at which dancers, singers, poets and musicians compete.

The breeding of sheep is an important industry in Wales and consequently wool is used extensively for clothing.

Plate 19 shows the Welsh woman's costume which would be made of wool, locally woven and dyed. The costume is not old in design, however, as it was evolved in the nineteenth century and based on those popular in the seventeenth and eighteenth centuries. The brown over-dress has a skirt which opens down the front, the edges of which are folded back to show the bright red underskirt, which is also in wool or flannel. The red dye was obtained from cockles and the brown dye from certain rock lichens.

The apron is woven in a fine wool or cotton check; there are many variations of colours. The tall black beaver hat is worn over a white frilled bonnet. The white blouse has broderie anglaise on the cuffs and a red ribbon is threaded through and tied at the wrists. Long underdrawers are also worn and decorated with broderie anglaise and ribbon.

The men wear breeches, usually of a dark colour, a waistcoat and a white shirt. Buckled shoes are worn by both men and women.

CORSICA

With the limited natural resources available, the costumes of Corsica have remained simple as well as being durable and practical and are unspoiled by modern or outside influences.

On the coast an Italian influence is evident, but in the remote mountain villages more sombre colours are worn. Women wear longish skirts and dark, long-sleeved blouses or tight fitting jackets. A black handkerchief or 'mezzaro' is draped on the head and black leather shoes are worn to resist the harsh mountain weather.

The shepherds and the men from the mountains wear black waistcoats and trousers made in hard-wearing corduroy or velveteen. There are many kinds of thick shirts, and broad red cummerbunds are also worn. Black berets or caps give protection to the head and strong black leather shoes protect the feet.

Several festivals are held in different parts of the island, and these occasions are opportunities to see the local costumes, one of which is illustrated in Plate 20. Black trousers and waistcoat are highlighted by the red sash and the coloured check overshirt. This smock type of shirt is gathered into a round narrow yoke and is worn tucked into the trousers. A similar form of smock is found in many countries although it is usually worn outside the trousers.

MALTA

Folk costume is only worn now in Malta at carnival time or on other special occasions. The very old dress called a Faldetta was worn by most of the townswomen, but is rarely seen now; this costume, peculiar to Malta, is reminiscent of the large cloaks worn in North Africa and is known as 'the hood of shame'. It consists of a long length of black silk material gathered on to a half circular wire frame. One end was held in the right hand and the frame formed a hood over the head, whilst the left hand held the material which was draped round the body like a cloak. It is believed to have come from Sicily or Spain at the time of the Arab invasions, when it was customary for the women to cover their faces.

The couple in Plate 20 are dressed in the costumes worn by folk groups today. They are based on those popular in the nineteenth century and reflect the Italian and Sicilian love of colour.

The woman's cotton skirt and blouse is not restricted to one colour and may be in stripes of light or dark blue or with horizontal stripes. The skirt opens down the front and is fastened with coloured bows. The blouse and apron are trimmed with finely made island lace of an intricate pattern. The headscarf, knotted at the back, can be in a contrasting colour or of the same material as the skirt.

The man can wear red, black, blue, white or striped trousers with a matching or contrasting waistcoat. He carried over his left shoulder a brightly striped scarf with pockets at each end. A sash in plain or striped cotton material is also usually worn. The stocking cap, which ends in a tassel, can also be in coloured stripes: it is typical of those worn by the fishermen of Malta. All are wearing leather shoes but sometimes they are replaced by sandals.

SARDINIA

The influences of several civilisations are reflected in the speech, customs and costumes of Sardinia.

The island is divided into four provinces and in each of these areas the costumes vary considerably.

There are numerous festivals, processions and equestrian displays, all of which are opportunities to display costumes, which are worn with great pride. Colours are very definite, such as red, white, black and brown with touches of blue, green and yellow, all of which express the unusual landscape of the island. Silver and gold is used in the making of bracelets, necklaces, chains, rings and filigree buttons. The latter vary in shape from town to town: in some villages they are made like the wild anisette or aniseed flower. The material used for clothing is the wool shorn from the island's sheep which is spun, dyed from recipes using local herbs and then woven by hand.

Floral designs only are used on costumes and the embroidery is executed in gold, silver and silk thread. A feature of the women's costumes are the beautiful skirts which are long, full and pleated. The old method of pleating known as 'fatta a tabellas' is still used. The pleats are loosely tacked in place and then the skirt is dipped into water and pressed under large stones. Many of the skirts are made in a button-through style with an opening on the right reaching from the waist to the hem; they are fastened with gold buttons.

Red is a popular colour for skirts and many have a deep band of embroidery at the hem. Sometimes this band is hand-painted with a floral design. The pleated skirt worn in Sennori is black and has a deep band of white, embroidered with flowers emphasised by a deep red band. The side opening is outlined with pale blue ribbon. In Orgosolo the skirt is brown with a band of green and red at the hem, and from the mountain village of Bitti the skirt has alternate bands of floral designs.

White sleeveless bodices cut high at the back and very low at the front are worn in several costumes; the very full sleeves are gathered into cuffs ending in deep frills.

In Seneghe the large sleeves are pleated, either horizontally or vertically, and are freshly pressed for each wearing. The costume from this village is very plain and devoid of embroidery, its main feature being the sleeves and the heavy gold necklaces set with pendants and precious stones, which cover the front of the blouse. Gold bracelets and rings on each finger are also worn. In one village each gold ring is fastened to a gold belt by a long chain.

In Villanova the blouse is red, and high-necked with long tight sleeves. Twelve bands of gold braid circle the arm from the elbow to the cuff, each ending with a gold button on the outside edge. Over this blouse is a bodice of very fine red and black stripes, edged with black. The red pleated skirt has a deep border of embroidery at the hem.

Very unusual jackets are to be found in Sardinia: the sleeve is made with only an outer section which fastens at the wrist over the full-sleeved blouse. This upper sleeve is decorated in many ways, ranging from gold braid bands to thickly encrusted gold thread embroidery. In Sennori the sleeve is also edged with a white lace frill and the blouse edged with pale blue.

Aprons vary considerably in size, colour and design, according to the village. They can be quite plain in black or brown or have a border of embroidery, either at the hem or around three sides. The apron can be of brocade and pleated or have wide bands of brocade on three sides and a red pleated centre panel, such as found near Cagliari. Lace aprons are also worn and a pale blue silk apron from Sennori is embroidered all over with flowers found on the island.

Head-dresses range from a simple white lace or linen draped mantilla to a type of red cape, edged in blue or a band of gold embroidery.

In Osilo, a copricappa or cape of red velvet with a deep white band of floral embroidery is worn. The thickness of the cape gives protection against the rain and the cold in this mountain village. A widow would wear a plain black cape and black pleated skirt, but with a red jacket.

The women of Ploaghe wear a blue and black brocaded cape with a large orange cross on the back dating from the fifteenth century, when a great plague swept through the island; the cross was invoked as a protection.

Head-dresses made of folded or draped white linen all have a piece of material which passes under the chin; at one time this would have covered the mouth in the belief that it was a protection from malaria.

At one time Sardinian women wore white hand-knitted stockings with beautifully embroidered shoes that matched their dresses. Now, red, black or white low-heeled shoes are worn.

Plate 21 shows a woman wearing a costume from Gavoi; her hand-pleated skirt is made with the pleats narrower at the waist and increasing in width towards the hem. Under the blue patterned bodice, the fine white cotton blouse has narrow tucks in the front. She also wears the cape or copricappa, on her head.

Men's costumes have not changed much since early times. The full white linen trousers, called burzighinos or crazzas are gathered into a pair of black gaiters or leggings. The trousers can also be worn like a divided skirt reaching to mid-calf and without being gathered at the knees. Over the trousers is a short, gathered, black skirt made from the local hard-wearing wool called orbace. An embroidered or plain leather belt holds the skirt in place. Waistcoats vary and can be single-breasted and made in brocade which has a dark background with a floral pattern or of black orbace. Gold buttons, either in one or two rows, fasten the waistcoats.

In Samugheo, in the province of Cagliari, black velvet waistcoats have a square neckline with a design painted on the front and the edges are bound in red. In some villages a plain, round-necked waistcoat with no front fastening is worn. Plate 21 shows a man wearing the traditional Nuorese costume.

Several waistcoats are made with sleeves and are really more like a jacket. The sleeve is split along the inner seam from the shoulder to the wrist, where it is buttoned. In Desulo this type of jacket is made in red orbace. In Oliena the jacket is red but the sleeves are made in a similar pattern to those worn by the women: this sleeve consists of only an upper section, which has a floral design on a white background, and the jacket is reversible and worn according to the occasion.

Long-sleeved black jackets are worn over dark waistcoats, but they do not have split sleeves. A thick, sleeveless fur coat made from goat or sheepskin and called a mastrucca, is made in various lengths and dyed black, brown or kept in its natural shade. In summer the fur is worn outside and in winter the fur is reversed.

White linen shirts have full sleeves and are fastened at the neck and cuffs with filigree buttons. In some villages the collar is worn down and in others it stands up and no ties or scarves are worn.

The traditional hat is a birritta, a long stocking type of hat made of orbace wool or felt (see Plate 21). It can be worn in various ways, with the end hanging down the back or on the left side of the face: it can also be folded or rolled back on the head, making a flat cap. The fishermen in the Cagliari wear a red birritta and the men from Teulada have a grey, Spanish type of sombrero.

Leggings or gaiters are made of black leather or thick black knitted wool and in some villages a red band is tied under the knee to keep the top of the legging in place. Shoes, which are laced, are of black leather.

SICILY

Numerous festivals are held throughout Sicily and the costumes worn on these occasions reveal the Sicilian's love of colour.

There are two types of costume, those that are truly Sicilian and those that derive from Albania.

The costumes illustrated in Plate 22 are from Piana degli Albanesi and show Albanian influence.

The women's full skirts are made of heavy silk taffeta and reach to the ground. Three very broad bands of gold embroidery encircle the skirt, or the skirt may be embroidered with a gold floral design.

The bodices are sleeveless, cut with low V necklines and the sides are embroidered with gold. Bodices and skirts are red, a colour which was believed to eliminate bad influences. A long narrow apron of black lace or a red apron covered with a gold design is worn over the skirt.

Blouses are white with wide sleeves and have a lace-edged collar which ends in a square panel at the back, not unlike a sailor's collar. On to this collar a deep lace frill is gathered.

The large, flat, green taffeta bow or rosette on the front of the bodice is embroidered with gold flowers and edged with gold. The heavy silver belt fastens with a large and elaborate silver buckle bearing the figure of St. George or the Odighitria Madonna worked in silver or gold. A blue cape is worn round the shoulders or over the head; when not in use, it is folded and carried over the arm. It is made of blue silk taffeta, lined and covered with gold embroidery and has a gold embroidered band. A narrow band of red material is folded and draped across the head. White stockings are worn with black leather shoes which have green bows.

Men wear thick white trousers which narrow down to the ankles and have a black or braided stripe running down the seams. A red sleeveless waistcoat and sleeveless jacket are both covered with a fine gold braid or embroidery. The white shirt has a line of embroidery round the stand-up collar, cuffs and down the front. The round pill box type of hat has a side flap ending in a red tassel. White shoes, not unlike those of the Greeks are worn; they have turned-up toes with red pom poms on the end.

Although the Albanians still maintain their own costumes, folk dances, traditions and religion, they are now integrated into the Sicilian background.

The Sicilian costume is far less complicated. Women wear full skirts of red, yellow, blue, pink or black, with several bands of coloured ribbons or braid round the lower half. In some areas small, semicircular or square aprons edged with braid or embroidery are worn: all are made in contrasting colours to the skirts. Bodices vary: there is a black velvet, strapless bodice laced or buttoned in the front which is worn rather like a corset. The bodice is cut high up to the bust line in front and fits well into the waist and on to the hips. This type of bodice is worn over a white blouse with a round low neck and full, three-quarter length sleeves. The brightly coloured skirt has a short apron of a contrasting colour. In Palermo the black velvet bodice fastens up the front to the bust line and has straps over the shoulder. The white blouse has a round neck and short sleeves. Brightly coloured skirts are worn without aprons and a scarf is tied over the head and knotted at the back.

Bodices are replaced in some areas by tightly fitting sleeved jackets with gold embroidery on the front. A dark red jacket and skirt can be worn with a white apron decorated with open-work embroidery; with these goes a high-necked white blouse. The jackets can be of contrasting colour to the skirts.

Hair is generally kept long, but head scarves are occasionally worn. Coral earrings and necklaces, beads and bracelets are added decoration. The stockings are white and the shoes of light black leather.

The men wear black or dark blue breeches fastened at the knee with silver buttons or red braid. Long-sleeved black jackets or coloured sleeveless waistcoats are worn over white, long-sleeved shirts which are fastened at the neck with a red bow. Red sashes are wound round the waist with the ends falling free. White stockings and lightweight black shoes are usual. The fishermen favour striped stockings with black, rolled-up trousers or loose breeches, a white shirt with a large, red, knotted scarf tied round the neck and a black or red stocking cap. Sometimes black leather boots or shoes are worn, but often they go barefooted.

THE BALEARIC ISLANDS

MAJORCA

The costumes of Majorca are simple, but individual and colourful. Women wear full skirts of plain cotton or brocade and these can have floral patterns, stripes or, if the skirt is of a plain colour, then a striped or plain apron in a contrasting colour is worn.

As in many other countries the colours reflect the landscape. Yellow and white stripes are very popular and deep blue and green, reflecting the sea, sky and olive groves.

A tight black bodice with three-quarter length sleeves and with a high round neckline adorns the upper part of the body and a very fine cotton or lace wimple frames the head and face, falling softly on to the shoulders. The head-dress is caught under the chin and buttoned down the front. White petticoats and long drawers are worn with white stockings and either flat black shoes or canvas or leather shoes with a low heel.

Men wear large, full baggy trousers gathered in at the knees. These can be striped or plain and are usually in shades of brown, dark orange, plum or blue. The waistcoats, in various colours, have brocaded fronts with plain backs. A wide sash with flowing ends is worn round the waist. Shirts are white and open-necked. A loosely knotted handkerchief with the point at the back is draped round the neck. White stockings and black shoes similar to those of the women are worn.

Plate 23 illustrates a couple from Majorca.

MINORCA

The basic costume of the Menorquins is very similar in style to those found on Majorca. The women wear full skirts with floral designs rather than stripes; the bodice is black, but the sleeves are long. The wimple style head-dress is made of the same material as the skirt, but is unusually long, covering shoulders, chest and the upper back.

White petticoats, white stockings and black leather shoes with a small heel and a decorative buckle make up the rest of the costume.

The men wear tight black knee breeches with a white, open-necked shirt, a coloured sash and a waistcoat either of a plain colour or in patterned brocade. The shoes are similar to those of the women. The island is renowned for its skill in shoe making.

IBIZA

The costumes worn in Ibiza bear no relation to those found in Minorca or Majorca.

The women wear very full long skirts in black, dark blue or white, often with accordion pleating. A matching blouse is worn with round gold buttons hanging from the sides of the sleeves. A very large fringed shawl is worn rather like a cape, covering the front and the sleeves of the blouse and reaching to a point down the back. The shawls are of a heavy dark brocade or embossed velvet. A short apron of black patterned silk or a tiny gold woven apron covered by a triangular white handkerchief is worn. An important feature of the women's costume is the wearing of numerous gold chains and necklaces. These signify the wealth of the wearer and are cherished heirlooms. Sometimes rings are worn on each finger and these are of a special square design and have little loose chains attached to each. A white or coloured scarf is tied under the chin and the hair is worn in a long plait at the back and tied with a large bow of coloured ribbons. Several long white petticoats are worn with white canvas alpargatas (rope-soled shoes) laced over black stockings. Plate 23 illustrates this costume.

The men wear thick white cotton trousers, baggy at the waist and gradually tapering down towards the ankle. Round the waist is a black or red sash with the ends tucked in. A black or red waistcoat with lapels has a stand-up collar and across the front are three rows of filigree buttons loosely clipped to the material. The long-sleeved white shirt also has a stand-up collar around which is tied a red scarf. A red stocking cap with a black head band is worn with the crown folded over one side. White canvas alpargatas are most popular and are worn with or without stockings.

SPAIN

Apart from the U.S.S.R., Spain has probably the greatest number of costumes to be found anywhere in Europe. The simplicity and austerity of some Spanish costumes compares vividly with the richness and brilliant colouring of others. Materials used range from velvets and brocades to satins, cotton and wool. The costumes of one province will bear no resemblance to those of its neighbours and even within a small area costumes can vary considerably.

Although several of the provinces are discussed in this book there is such a wealth of costumes that only the most popular are described.

ANDALUSIA

It was in this region that Flamenco music and dancing developed and became synonymous with Spain. There are two types of dresses for flamenco dancing: one, a short flounced dress and the other a dress with a long train or tail. The short dress has a tight fitting bodice reaching to the hips with a full skirt of three or four layers of frills. With this is worn a white starched cotton petticoat with layers of frills inside it. The dress can be of a spotted cotton material in a variety of colours or can be plain or floral patterned. The popularity of the dance has brought many variations and elaborate designs involving net, lace, taffeta and other fabrics. This costume is not worn by dancers alone but can be seen generally at the Easter Fair at Seville.

The long tailed dress is worn only by dancers when performing some of the slow, sustained dances such as the Alegrias or Soleares. The frills of the dress are starched or lined to give them a stiffness, and manipulating this costume is a great art; Plate 24 shows this dress. Originally made in a plain or spotted cotton, it is now designed using many different materials. The shoes worn have very strong heels which are essential for the foot beats and are between 50 and 75 mm in height. They usually match the dress, but red is now a very popular colour.

The man wears very tight fitting trousers cut well above the waist, with a chaleco or short waistcoat and a short jacket (see Plate 24). Alternatively there can be a spotted long-sleeved blouse which ties over the trousers. Black is the usual colour for the trousers with the jackets and waistcoats in a variety of colours, these being adopted for theatrical purposes. The flat crowned, straight brimmed Cordobés hats are popular with all Andalusian men as they give good protection from the sun. A common practice in the making of shoes is to have small nails with large heads hammered into the heels to give a flat metal surface. Sometimes a metal plate is attached to the heels and toecaps to give a stronger sound to the beats of the dancers.

VALENCIA

The women's costumes are made of silk floral brocade in pastel shades. An apron and fichu of fine lace embroidered with gold are worn. A large pink or blue bow keeps the fichu in place at the back, with another large bow to fasten the apron. The hair is dressed in a special style peculiar only to this province, with a large plaited bun at the back with two smaller buns in 'earphone' style at the sides. A large gold comb is fixed into the large bun with two smaller combs in each of the other buns. Large pins decorated with pearls and jewels are fixed into the hair and gold earrings are also worn. White stockings and white shoes with small heels are worn.

Men wear tight knee breeches with long-sleeved short jackets made in pale blue satin. A red sash is worn with a white shirt and white stockings are worn with alpargatas (rope-soled shoes) which are laced and tied round the ankles. The hat is a pale blue or white knitted skull cap which has a series of tassels hanging down from the crown. There is also a long multi-coloured striped shawl or rug, which is draped over the shoulders. Occasionally men wear an older costume which has links with ancient Greece. This has short trousers made of white linen, pleated resembling a divided skirt. A red sash is tied round the waist and an embroidered or brocaded sleeveless waistcoat is worn over a long-sleeved white shirt. A red or striped scarf, similar to a turban, is wrapped round the head. White or blue stockings are worn.

CATALONIA

Women wear full skirts of a pastel shade with floral designs on them. The black satin bodice is edged with white lace and a white or black lace shawl is draped round the shoulders. Aprons vary and can be small and of black lace or larger in white with silk embroidery or trimmed with lace. Black lace mittens and a large black hair net or snood is worn on the head. White stockings and either a low-heeled black shoe or alpargatas are worn.

The men wear tight black knee breeches with a black jacket and a white shirt with a red sash round the waist. The red cap is similar to the stocking cap or phrygian so popular round the Mediterranean. In Catalonia the men fold the crown under in the front. Alpargatas are laced round the ankle and up the legs over the white stockings.

ARAGON

This large province in the north-east is well known for its songs and dances, especially the Jota.

The costumes used for this dance are illustrated in Plate 25. The woman's gathered skirt is in cotton and usually has a dark or black background with a floral design, but now lighter colours are worn. The bodice is in black velvet and covered with a fringed shawl which crosses

Italian 'tovaglia'

Bamboo or straw hat from the Far East

Masked head-dress from Fano, Denmark

Sheepskin hat worn in Eastern Europe

Breton lace coif, France

Tehuana lace head-dress from Mexico

German 'halsmantel'
or 'halsband'

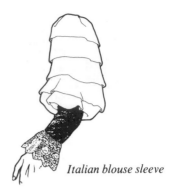

Italian blouse sleeve

Swedish pocket

A 'tight wrap' from
Spakenburg,
Netherlands

Yemeni head-dress

over in front and ties at the back. The apron is in black silk. White knitted stockings are worn with rope-soled alpargatas which have canvas tops and are tied with black tapes.

The man wears trousers and a velvet or corduroy jacket with white cotton under-trousers or pololos. The sash and head band are in red wool. The very broad sash was once used as a pocket, but is now purely decorative.

BASQUE

Apart from one or two exceptions, the costumes of the Basques are simple. The women wear a full red skirt with black bands round the hem and a plain black apron over it. A white, high-necked and long-sleeved blouse is worn under a black sleeveless bodice which is laced up the front. Alpargatas are laced up the leg over white stockings. The head is covered with a white handkerchief knotted at the back.

The men's costume is not unlike that of the English Morris dancers, with whom they have a similarity of movement in their dancing. Trousers and shirt are white with a red sash round the waist. A red beret is worn and, on the feet, alpargatas are laced in red round the ankles.

GALICIA

The women in Galicia wear full red skirts with one or two bands of black velvet round the hem, similar in style to those in other northern provinces. Over the skirt is either a small black apron decorated with black lace and jet beads, or a large apron completely covering the skirt. A type of cross-over shawl is worn tied at the back and this can be red or black, with a band of velvet and jet beads, though in some villages it is of white lace. The blouse is high-necked with long sleeves. A yellow or white handkerchief is tied round the head and knotted on the top. Materials used are heavy, unlike the cotton used in the south.

Men wear black trousers to below the knees and under these are white under-trousers, or pololos, which are tucked into the tops of high black gaiters. Silver buttons fasten the gaiters on the sides and there are also buttons on the outside trousers at the knees. A white open-necked shirt is worn with a waistcoat which is black in front, but has a plain coloured back. A wide red sash is tied round the waist. There are black lace-up shoes and a triangular shaped hat reaching to a point with a red pom pom on top. The costumes of both the men and the women vary in colour and design from one district to another.

PORTUGAL

The many festivals of the Portuguese reveal a strong national spirit as well as their ability to express enjoyment and happiness. This exuberance is seen in their bright and colourful costumes and even the fisherman's garb is far from being sombre.

The women's skirts throughout Portugal are fairly full. Complicated head-dresses are not worn: scarves are draped loosely over the head with black felt hats on top; this has a flat crown and is used for carrying articles on the head. The hat is sometimes replaced by a pad, known as a mother-in-law.

In the coastal areas shoes are rarely worn, except on special occasions when either shoes or backless mules are used.

The most colourful of the women's costumes are from Vianna do Castelo in the Minho region, one of which is illustrated in Plate 26. The skirt is made of homespun linen and wool woven into stripes of red, yellow, white, green and black with red as the predominating colour. This costume has a deep border of black with white embroidery in wool. The bodice, partly hidden by the shawl, has an upper section in red and the lower part in black, both parts being embroidered with coloured wools. The bodice laces up the front and is worn over a white linen, long-sleeved blouse with blue embroidery at the neck, cuffs and upper sleeves.

The apron has an upper section which is very finely gathered and forms a plain band. The lower half is covered with a pattern either woven into the material or embroidered on to it. The ends of the shawl are tucked into the waistband and a scarf in similar pattern is tied round the head. Shawls and scarves can vary in colour from village to village.

White petticoats are worn and white knee-length stockings in a lacy pattern: sometimes the stockings are footless. The slip-on mules have beautifully embroidered uppers.

Gold chains, pendants, coins, crosses and hearts, together with other filigree ornaments, are very popular in this region. The costume from Vianna do Castelo is also made with blue as the underlying colour. This is not quite so popular, but is in the same style as illustrated, with dark blue predominant and a lighter blue, yellow and white used in the stripes and the embroidery. Sometimes the skirt is white with a dark blue border, apron and a bodice of contrasting blues, or a white skirt with a red border and a black and red bodice.

A bride on her wedding day wears a black dress of velvet with an apron beautifully embroidered with gold and jet beads. On her head is a white lace mantilla and round her neck many gold chains and other ornaments.

The man's costume from Vianna do Castelo (Plate 26) consists of a black suit with a curved line of white buttons on the jacket and sleeves. A red sash is tied round the waist. Shoes are of black leather. This costume provides a strong contrast to the very bright colours worn by the women.

In lower Minho and the regions below the Douro, the women wear full gathered skirts of red, pink or other coloured cotton and round the hips a broad red or black sash. This gives a curious line with a slight balloon effect between waist and hip. Over a white or coloured long-sleeved blouse a brightly coloured floral shawl is worn with the ends caught at the waist. A black felt hat with a brim is worn over a plain or coloured scarf.

In Esposende a little mirror is fixed into the hat band: as the women waited on the shore for the fishing boats to arrive, the mirrors flashed in the sun which helped the fishermen to guide their boats home.

The costumes from the fishing village of Nazare are known for the use of tartan. Each family has a different pattern and it is thought that tartan was brought by the Scottish soldiers who fought in the Peninsular wars in the early nineteenth century. The Portuguese admired the tartan and wove their own patterns. The women in this area wear a gathered tartan skirt with either a plain or tartan apron which may be short or fairly long. The simple short, or rolled-up, sleeved blouse can be white, floral or coloured. A floral or black scarf is draped over the head. The hat is a round black felt with a 'pork pie' crown with a large black pom-pom on the side.

In the Algarve, skirts are red, blue, yellow, pink or green with two or three bands of coloured braid, and are full. The cotton blouse has a puffed upper sleeve gathered into a tight fitting lower section, a high round neck and a type of large collar or cape edged with lace. The colours for the blouses vary from plain blue, yellow and pink to floral patterns on a white base. The blouse is worn outside the skirt like a jacket and when the short apron is tied round the waist it gives a fluted appearance to the blouse hem.

A black felt brimmed hat, rather like a Spanish hat, is worn over a scarf with a floral design and a flower is fixed into the hat band. Several white petticoats are worn with white knitted stockings and laced-up leather boots. Plate 27 illustrates a woman from the Algarve.

One of the most interesting of the men's costumes comes from Nazare, where the fishermen go barefooted and wear the tartan shirts and trousers so popular in this area. On their heads a black stocking cap is worn.

On the southern side of the Tagus are the lowlands of the Ribatejo, the centre of bull breeding. Here the men spend their lives in the saddle and are known as campinos. They wear distinctive costumes of black or brown knee breeches which have four gold buttons at the knee and three at the hip pocket. A sleeveless red waistcoat is worn over a white long-sleeved shirt complete with a red sash with the ends tucked in. A special green and red stocking cap, the verdegaio, is worn only by the campinos. The stockings are white and the shoes black.

The costume of the Algarve is very simple: black trousers, black sleeveless waistcoat, white shirt and black stockings (see Plate 27). The shoes are of black leather and a cap ending in a tassel may be worn.

Two very unusual costumes are found in Portugal, one from Miranda do Douro in the province of Tras os Montes. Here the men wear a white, three tiered skirt with frilled and embroidered edges. A brightly coloured scarf is tied round the waist with the ends hanging down. A black waistcoat is worn over a long-sleeved white shirt buttoned to the neck. Round the shoulders is draped a floral shawl with a fringed edge. A black felt hat is worn, decorated with flowers and ribbons. The stockings have a horizontal striped design and the ankle boots are black. This costume is only worn when a particular dance, similar to the English Morris, is executed.

The other unusual costume is only worn in July by the Sargaceiros, or seaweed gatherers, at Apulia (Minho). A white woollen, long-sleeved coat or tunic reaching to below the thighs is fastened with a broad leather belt. Short trousers are worn under this and on the head a type of sou'wester, rather like a Roman helmet.

MADEIRA

The costume of Madeira is simple, but colourful. The women wear full red wool skirts with yellow, black, white or green stripes which are woven into the material. A red bodice embroidered in yellow and laced up the front is worn with a white linen blouse with short sleeves. A little red cape is draped round the shoulders, or over the left shoulder if not required for warmth or protection from the weather.

The head-dress is simple also and is a type of blue skull cap ending in a point. Boots are made of white or red soft leather. The women's costume of Madeira is shown in Plate 27.

The men wear a loose, white, cotton or linen long-sleeved shirt. Loose, wide trousers are white, calf length and gathered into a band or cuff which fastens with white buttons.

A broad white or red sash is tied at the waist and a similar type of cap to those of the women is worn, except that it has two triangular pieces at the sides in the headgear.

White boots are worn without stockings.

THE CANARY ISLANDS

The colourful costumes of the Canary Islands reflect their scenic beauty. The materials used are hand woven from a hard wearing wool and the embroidery and drawn thread work is very fine; each island has created its own design incorporating floral motifs. There are numerous festivals, and these are the occasions when costumes are worn.

TENERIFE

On this island the women wear colourful striped skirts similar to those seen in Madeira. There is a great variety in colour as the material is woven individually at home. White petticoats are worn and these have fine drawn thread work at the hems. Sometimes the skirt is drawn up on one side in order to display the petticoat's beautiful handiwork. A black or red laced-up bodice is worn together with a white blouse, high necked and with puff sleeves. The bodice is edged with red or yellow and has a scalloped edge in squares. A little white or yellow flat straw hat, edged with red, is worn over a white or yellow scarf tied under the chin or at the back of the head. A small white apron and white stockings with little black ankle boots complete the costume, although the boots are now sometimes replaced by black shoes. Plate 28 shows a little girl wearing this costume.

The men wear black trousers which come to the knees, worn over a loose pair of white under-trousers. A side opening at the knee is laced up in red with red pom-poms. The red waistcoat edged with yellow has a white back and the open necked shirt is also white. A red sash is tied round the waist with long fringed edges falling on the left side. Black shoes are worn and white stockings now often replace gaiters.

GRAND CANARY

The women wear large, white, pale blue, red or green skirts which are tucked up each side to give a pannier effect found in the costumes of the late eighteenth century. Plate 28 illustrates this costume. The edge of the skirt has a deep border or several bands of drawn thread work. The under-skirt can be either red, pale blue or yellow and has a deep band of embroidery in a geometrical design. There is a great variation in these bands and designs and each skirt is different. A popular colour combination is a white skirt worn with a red under-skirt, or this can be red and blue or blue and yellow. A fine lawn white apron edged with a border of drawn thread work is worn over the draped skirt. A long-sleeved white jacket with a high round neck has a square edged hem line and the front is decorated with a fine drawn thread embroidery. White rather than coloured jackets are the general rule. Little black felt hats are worn over white, red or pale blue silk head scarves, which either hang loosely down the back or are knotted into a type of bow. White stockings are worn with low heeled black shoes, with a pom pom or a folded ribbon at the front. As the skirts are long and weighed down with the weight of the embroidery, numerous petticoats are not required.

The men wear white linen pleated trousers cut like a divided skirt, a costume similar to that seen in Valencia. A white open-necked shirt has large full sleeves gathered into a band at the elbow. A red or black waistcoat has a plain white or pale coloured back and a black sash is worn round the waist. There are upper socks which only cover the calves, after which there is a gap and small white ankle socks which are folded over the tops of light brown ankle boots. A black felt, wide brimmed hat is worn, but discarded during dancing, or allowed to hang down the back suspended on a cord. This costume is also illustrated in Plate 28.

CZECHOSLOVAKIA

The dances, folklore and costumes of Czechoslovakia overlap the borders of the country, but there is a marked difference between costumes from Bohemia and those of Slovakia, or those of the plains as compared with those of the people from the Tatra mountains.

BOHEMIA

Bohemia has had many cultural contacts with Austria and the west so that the costumes show strong western influences. The women's skirts are often pleated and are dark red or black in colour, with an embroidered border at the hem. These pleats are made by wetting the material, pressing in the pleats, tying up the skirts and putting them out to.dry. Plain or striped skirts are worn with large white aprons, which are decorated with white embroidery and edged with white lace. In some districts aprons made in striped floral brocade, reaching to the hem of the skirt and covering part of the back, are worn. Black bodices are neat and cut rather low in the front and are worn over white blouses with elbow-length full puff sleeves and high, round, frilled necklines. In some areas a floral patterned shawl is draped over the bodice completely covering it and with the ends tucked into the apron.

Unmarried girls usually have their hair in a long plait down the back and a black velvet decorated head band. Married woman wear neat little bonnets with a decorated or plain bow at the back. In some villages a beautifully embroidered black scarf or Satek is tied on the head. Several white petticoats are worn, with red knitted cotton stockings and black, low heeled shoes: these sometimes have embroidered uppers or a rosette of ribbons.

The men wear yellow cloth or buckskin knee-length breeches with white stockings and black leather shoes or boots. Dark blue or black waistcoats have embroidered small stand-up collars. Down the edge of the waistcoats are rows of silver buttons. The white shirt has an embroidered front in white stitching with full sleeves gathered into the cuffs and with a turn-down collar: this shirt is sometimes worn with a coloured knotted scarf or tie. Black felt hats with rather large brims, or round fur hats with a crown of wool or felt, are worn.

Plate 29 shows a couple dancing in the costumes of Bohemia.

MORAVIA

Towards the east costumes become more elaborate, Women's skirts are fuller and made from floral patterned materials which are also used for the aprons. Skirts are also made in pastel shades of pink, yellow, blue or white, and are either gathered or finely pleated. The white, blue, black or yellow aprons are more elaborate and the bodices are decorated with embroidery. White blouses tend to have larger sleeves and the frill at the neck has a heavier emphasis. Embroidery using black or gold thread is used on the blouses and ribbons are used for decoration. The hair is plaited in a long tail with ribbons or a handkerchief tied over the head. Tight-fitting little bonnets are worn at the back of the head and also decorated with ribbons. Unmarried girls have the plait of hair down the back, married women tuck their hair out of sight. White or black stockings are worn with black boots or low heeled shoes.

The men wear tight black, blue or red trousers with braiding on the sides, front and across the back. The white linen shirts have loose wide sleeves, embroidered or decorated with drawn thread work. The waistcoats vary and can be red, edged with gold braid and gold buttons, or of the small bolero type made either of brocade, embroidered, or black and decorated with large red pom-poms. Two leather belts are worn across the waist and hips, and tucked into the belt or trouser pocket is a beautifully embroidered handkerchief which has been made and presented by a girl friend. Boots are black and round black hats with rolled brims are decorated with bunches of flowers and white feathers. The feathers are difficult to find and there is great competition among the young men to obtain them. The wearing of this feather is a sign of manhood, but once married the feather is put away.

SLOVAKIA

The remoteness of Slovakia has helped to preserve its individuality. Costumes have two different styles, that of the people of the Tatra mountains and that of the people of the plains.

The women of the mountain regions wear a much simpler style with less petticoats, plain or floral patterned skirts, blouses of heavy linen with less embroidery and white stockings with soft leather flat shoes tied round the ankles. The women of the plains have more patterned skirts, elaborate aprons and bodices of embroidery and braid. White caps embroidered in red and black on the crown and sides fit tightly on to the head. Little caps with bows and ribbons are also worn and the hair is also plaited with ribbons. White stockings with black boots are usual.

The men from the Tatra mountains wear loose fitting white linen trousers reaching to the calf with the ends of the trousers fringed. A broad leather belt is worn and the shirt has wide-ended sleeves and a round neckline. In summer the shirt ends at the chest leaving a bare midriff. A short white leather waistcoat edged with black fur and embroidered with appliqué work is worn over the shirt. Leather sandals have black leather laces tied round the ankles over white socks. A very small black round hat with a tiny brim is worn. In the region near the Polish border, thick white long trousers are worn with a deep leather belt, a white shirt with full loose sleeves and a black hat which has a wide turned-up brim. Soft leather shoes are laced up round the ankles over the trousers.

The men from west Slovakia wear long white trousers tucked into black boots with elaborate braiding on the front of the trousers. The waistcoats are longer than those of Moravia and are often plain, but can be decorated with braid and buttons. White high-necked shirts with wide loose sleeves are worn with a studded belt.

POLAND

Throughout its troubled history, Poland has kept its strong national identity and yet shows the cultures of both the east and the west.

The costumes are very individual and each region has its own style. In the villages great pride used to be put into the making of the costumes, with each family weaving the material on its own looms. Wool, flax and hemp were chiefly used and textiles were hard wearing. In some areas striped materials used in the making of women's skirts and men's trousers are traditional. There is a strong love of colour and the stripes are in red, yellow, green, orange, blue and mauve, all of which are used to good effect.

Lowicz is particularly famous for its striped woollen material and costumes from here are illustrated in Plate 30. The women's skirts are full and gathered rather than pleated, and are worn over several petticoats. High-necked bodices are embroidered with floral designs in silk or wool. In some areas gold and silver thread is used together with beads. In Krakow the bodice is decorated with braid, red beads and tassels (see Plate 31). Blouses are white, usually with long sleeves and varying necklines or small frilled collars. From region to region details change considerably and a very characteristic feature showing variation in costume is the apron. Red or black laced-up boots are worn a great deal in Poland. In the mountain areas a soft leather moccasin type of shoe, called a 'kierpce', is laced up round the ankles.

Young girls have their hair uncovered and worn in two plaits tied at the end with ribbons. Floral wreaths are also worn, or headscarves. Married women have their hair tucked into caps. Strings of beads are worn which can be of coral, glass or wood and, in the Baltic region, of amber or 'sun stone'.

The men's costumes are as colourful as the women's, with striped or plain coloured trousers tucked into red or black boots. In the Krakow area, for example, the trousers are in red and white or blue stripes (see Plate 31). The agriculture of the region of Lowicz is reflected in orange, gold and green (Plate 30). Shirts are white with long sleeves ending in cuffs and these are worn with sleeveless waistcoats. There is a great variety of jackets which are of various lengths, colours and styles. In the Krakow region the sleeveless coats are blue and reach to the knees. North of the region at Opoezno they are white and have sleeves. Further north in the Mazury province they are black.

Many of the men's costumes have a military cut and appearance, which may be the influence of the constant wars undergone by the country. Plate 31 illustrates a coat with gold braid trimmings and tassels based on Hussar uniform. The Poles are also a horse-riding nation, hence their full trousers and boots.

Red boots are now often worn by folk dance groups, but this is a modern innovation, black being more suitable to the military environment from which the costume developed. Plate 31 shows the man's attractive costume from Krakow.

A black felt hat with a shallow brim is popular in many regions and there is also a very decorative hat in the Krakow region which has a square red crown gathered into a black astrakan band. On the left of this hat is a peacock's feather which is regarded as a symbol of good luck.

In the region of the Tatra mountains in the south the costume varies a great deal from the rest of the country. The women wear green or tan coloured skirts which are covered with floral patterns. A tight fitting sleeveless embroidered velvet bodice, laced up in the front, has a basque at the waist, and is usually tan. A white, long-sleeved blouse is worn with rows of multi-coloured beads. The stockings are white and the leather 'kierpce' are laced round the ankles. The hair is tied back with a ribbon.

The men wear thick white woollen trousers which have black braid down the seams and across the back. On the front is a design in red, blue or black called 'parzenica' and each mountaineer has his own design. A long-sleeved shirt is fastened at the neck and has a brass brooch on the chest. A very wide leather belt of about 25 cm (10 in), studded with brass studs and several buckles, is worn. A black felt hat has a band of white mussel shells and an eagle or falcon's feather on the side. A fur lined white coat or cape is worn and is turned inside out in bad weather to protect the embroidery.

HUNGARY

Hungarian costumes are among the most beautiful in Europe and are distinguished by their colours, the use of embroidery, very full skirts, layers of petticoats and the full, white, divided skirt type of trousers worn by the men.

Many of the women's skirts are of finely pleated cotton or linen, either plain or in floral designs. In the north region of Buják, a short pleated skirt is worn with eight or nine starched petticoats giving a very bulky effect. A round-necked, sleeveless bodice, made in a white material with a floral pattern, is worn over a white blouse which has gathered sleeves caught just above the elbow with ribbons. Several blouses have full pleated sleeves which are starched, thus giving them an exaggerated shape. A white apron is embroidered with open-work stitching which is very popular in Hungary. Married women wear their hair in a bun, tucked into little scarves or caps. A dozen or more rows of light coloured beads are worn.

A costume derived from a wedding dress comes from the Matra mountains region. A white pleated skirt is worn over several petticoats: the bodice is pale blue and a white shawl decorated with open-work embroidery crosses over and ties at the back. A white, tight fitting, open-work cap is embroidered or decorated with flowers and has a bunch of floral ribbons falling down the back. White stockings are usually worn with black shoes or boots.

In the west and south, very elaborate floral patterned cotton skirts in various shades of green, blue and red cotton are worn (see Plate 33). Over the skirts, which can be pleated or gathered, are equally elaborate floral aprons, ending in a deep fringe. Bands of embroidered braid decorate the skirt and aprons. Géderlak in the central region is an area famous for its embroideries (see Plate 32).

A fringed shawl in a coloured pattern is often worn over a white, short-sleeved blouse. In some regions the blouse is worn without the shawl and gathered into the neck with a coloured bow. In the south, a dark bodice, laced up the front, is worn over the blouse.

The most elaborate and colourful costumes are from Mezőkövesd, in the north-east, where the skirts are tightly fitting from the waist to the hip then, from a band of embroidery, the lower half is finely gathered. Round the hem of the skirt are several coloured bands of braid. Floral patterned materials, popular in so many Hungarian regions, are used for the skirts. A long black apron of silk or velvet reaches to the hem of the skirt and is embroidered with flowers and braid. A jacket with a high round neck has little gathered sleeves and a basque, which is fluted and covered with embroidery. White stockings with black shoes are worn. Unmarried girls have their hair in plaits, but married women have tight scarves round their heads, on to which are fastened large, white woollen pom-poms. At one time the wool was brushed so that it looked like hair that had been back-combed.

The men's costumes can be divided into two styles. In many regions tight black trousers are tucked into black boots and worn with white shirts which have long sleeves, either wide and open-ended or gathered into cuffs (see Plate 33). Occasionally the shirt is worn outside the trousers like a tunic. Black sleeveless waistcoats with one or two rows of silver or gold buttons are worn. In the winter, long-sleeved black jackets are very popular. In many areas black felt hats are worn; these can have black or braided bands round the crown or coloured ribbons with the ends hanging down the back.

The most popular and alternative costume is that consisting of a white linen divided skirt or trousers, called gatya (see Plate 32). These reach to the calf and sometimes have a fringed edge. In Koppányszánto they are very full and gathered at the waist: in the west they are often very finely pleated. In some regions a black apron is worn, reaching to the edge of the trousers or skirt. In Nagybaracska, the aprons are woven in stripes, but in most areas they are embroidered.

The most decorative costume comes from Mezőkövesd and is worn only on special occasions such as at the conclusion of harvesting. Full white gatya trousers are worn with black aprons heavily embroidered and decorated with coloured braid. The shoulders, wide sleeves and front panels of the shirts are embroidered with flowers and braid. Black waistcoats are worn over the shirts and small brimmed, high domed hats are decorated with a broad black ribbon edged with yellow.

An interesting costume is worn by the shepherds and horsemen of the Hortobágy region. Here the linen gatya trousers are dyed a dark blue. A blue shirt with long wide sleeves has a turned-down collar. A black waistcoat with a round neck fastens with a row of silver or plain buttons.

A black felt hat with a wide turned-up brim is worn; it also has a chin strap.

A large white or saffron coloured felt coat, or szur, lined with sheep's wool, is worn like a cloak and the sleeves are sewn up and used only for decoration, or as pockets. These long coats, which reach to the calf, are decorated with braid and appliqué work. They are also made in sheepskin and are known as suba.

U.S.S.R.

There are thousands of costumes in the U.S.S.R. with not only the difference between urban and rural styles, but variations within respective areas.

RUSSIA—THE R.S.F.S.R.

The Russians have always woven their own materials for their costumes and are well known for their beautiful embroidery: each region has its own special design. One of the most elegant costumes from this region is the woman's sarafan, which is a type of pinafore dress and is illustrated in Plate 36 This is made in red, blue or gold and is either in brocade or a plain material. Gold or coloured braiding runs down the front and along the top of the bodice and the hem. The white blouse has a round neck and full three-quarter or full length sleeves which are often embroidered. The sarafan can also be worn short, reaching to just below the knees with petticoats underneath.

The crown type of head-dress, or kokoshnik, has a large bow at the back; formerly this headdress was elaborately decorated with pearls and jewels. Stockings are flesh coloured or white with either red boots or shoes.

A loose fitting smock type of shirt is worn by the men; overlapping the trousers it has a red cord tied round the waist. Full sleeves are gathered into embroidered cuffs and there is a band of embroidery round the high, stand-up collar and down the shirt opening on the left side, as well as along the hem. White or red linen is most popular for these shirts. Black, slightly full trousers which are tucked into black boots are found in the Moscow areas.

THE UKRAINE S.S.R.

The Ukrainians have a highly developed national sense, shown in their songs, dances and costumes. Plate 36 illustrates Ukrainian costume.

The women's costume is very attractive with its slim line and highly individual style. A short skirt of woven woollen material is worn over a tight white petticoat, which shows several inches below the skirt; this can be made in a two-colour design of squares in red, blues, yellows and greens and is tied round the waist. Since it has no front centre seam a white embroidered apron is worn over it. The velvet or woollen sleeveless jacket is in dark red, green or blue; it crosses over and fastens on the left side. The edges of the jacket, hem and neck have a band of embroidery or braid. A white blouse with full three-quarter length sleeves also has embroidery on the sleeves in a floral design. When the costume is worn without the jacket, a central panel of embroidery is shown on the blouse. The floral head-dress has long ribbons hanging down the back, and several rows of coloured beads are worn round the neck. Red boots complete this costume.

Very full red, white or blue trousers tucked into red boots, are worn by the men. A white linen shirt is worn inside the trousers with embroidery on the centre opening, round the neck and on the edge of the cuffs. A wide red, green or blue sash is tied round the waist and the two ends fall loosely on either side of the body. A fur cap of grey or white astrakan is often worn.

BYELORUSSIA (WHITE RUSSIA)

The attitude and strength of character of the White Russians is shown in their costumes, which are among the brightest to be found in the Soviet Union.

The women's full skirts are made in a pattern of red, white, blue, yellow, brown or green, woven into designs similar to those of a tartan. The white linen blouse, full sleeved, is gathered into frilled cuffs. The sleeves, small collar and the front of the blouse, together with a white apron, are all embroidered in a red geometrical design. A sleeveless red or dark brown jacket can either lace up the front with a red cord or be buttoned. A long white scarf is tied round the head with embroidered ends hanging down the back. Several white petticoats are worn with white or flesh coloured stockings and red, black or dark brown laced-up ankle boots. The costume is illustrated in Plate 35.

The men wear a white shirt with full sleeves and cuffs; the stand-up collar, front centre panels, edges and cuffs are all embroidered with a red geometrical design. The shirt is worn outside the trousers, which are fairly full and in stripes of red, brown, black or green. The trousers are tucked into black or brown boots and a narrow red sash is tied round the waist.

MOLDAVIA

Moldavians have a love of colour and embroidery which is shown in their costumes.

The women's costumes have several variations. The full skirt can be white, red or black, and pleated; it has a deep embroidered band at the hem. Two aprons are often worn, front and back; these are woven in bright horizontal stripes, a style which is also popular in Romania. A white linen, long-sleeved blouse has a block of red and blue embroidery across the upper sleeve or with lines of embroidery down the sleeves. Short white bolero jackets have embroidery on the neck, armholes and the lower edge and sometimes beads are used for decoration. A white or red handkerchief is tied at the back of the head or a posy of flowers at the side. Several petticoats, pale stockings, red or black boots, low heeled shoes or laced-up Romanian style sandals are worn. A costume from Moldavia is shown in Plate 37.

Men have white or black trousers tucked into black boots. A white shirt is worn outside the trousers and this has red or blue embroidery round the neck, down the front and on the edge of the long loose sleeves. A red sash with two loose ends on either side or a broad leather belt is worn round the waist. A heavily embroidered white or black leather sleeveless jacket is worn. A black or grey astrakan hat is worn on the back of the head.

THE BALTIC REPUBLICS

ESTONIA

Estonia, a land full of songs, dances and folklore, has some very colourful costumes.

In common with other northern countries, stripes are very popular with either deep horizontal bands round the skirts or fine downward stripes. The skirts are woven in a heavy material and are gathered at the waist or have very fine tucks. Dark red is a popular colour, but they may be in black, yellow or orange. Sleeveless bodices are worn with some costumes; and they are decorated and fastened with silver rosette clips. A white, long-sleeved blouse is gathered into cuffs and a wide, lace-edged collar is fastened with a brooch. Plate 34 shows a costume of this type.

When a perpendicular striped skirt is worn it is partnered with a heavy apron in the same shade. A black belt with a silver buckle holds the apron and skirt in place. No bodice is worn, but the blouse has red and blue embroidery along the top of the shoulders, round the collar and on the cuffs. A very tiny hat just sits on the top of the head. White stockings are usually worn, but there are also gaily coloured striped or patterned stockings to the knees. Black shoes sometimes have a decorated tongue over the instep. Some costumes have a loose pocket fixed on to a belt, as is found in Scandinavian countries.

The men wear black breeches, fastening at the knees with silver buttons, with a patterned or dark waistcoat, and a white, long-sleeved shirt fastened at the neck with a braided tie or brooch. A braided belt has two long ends and sometimes a skull cap is worn. Stockings are white, either plain or with a design, and the shoes are black.

LATVIA

The costumes of Latvia, of which there are several, are very different from neighbouring countries. One of the most attractive worn by the women has a full long skirt in dark blue or black with a deep border of red, composed of old Nordic patterns in embroidery (see Plate 34). The red sleeveless bodice has an unusual design worked in silver braid and the blouse has loose sleeves and a little turned-down collar. There is fine black embroidery around the shoulder seams, collar, neck opening and sleeve edges. A decorated round crown in silver, gold and red is worn on the head. Large antique, round, silver ornaments fasten the neck of the blouse and also hold in place, on the left shoulder, a cream cloak worn like the draped plaid of the Scots. White stockings and black shoes are worn.

Men wear long, calf-length white or cream coats embroidered down the front edge in black. Long white or cream trousers are gathered into white or coloured patterned ankle bands. Shoes are black, the socks white and the white shirt has a turned-down collar with a knotted braid bow. A long braid belt is tied round the coat.

LITHUANIA

Lithuania has several costumes and some of the most attractive are in shades of blue as shown in Plate 35. Long, hand-woven skirts in horizontal bands and stripes are worn with striped, sleeveless jackets reaching to the hips. A long braided belt can also be worn. Aprons are varied in design, and can be white with blue embroidered bands and a white fringe at the hem, or blue and red in design on a pale blue background, with a red fringe. A white blouse with full sleeves gathered into cuffs and with a little turned-down collar is worn. The lower sleeves, cuffs, collar and blouse front are embroidered in blue. In common with Latvia, little crowns are worn which are decorated with blue and red braid. Shoes are white, blue or natural leather, have cross-over straps round the ankles and are worn with white stockings.

The men wear pale blue, grey or striped trousers which end in an ankle cuff or band. A grey or blue sleeveless jacket is worn over a long-sleeved white shirt with cuffs. The jacket fastens at the waist with two buttons, and the edge armholes are decorated with braiding. A coloured braid belt with fringed ends is tied round the waist, under the jacket. The shirt cuffs are embroidered and a braided, knotted tie is worn. White socks are worn and the shoes are similar to those of the women with cross-over straps round the ankles.

THE CAUCASUS

Asian influence is shown in the costumes, especially in those of the women which are made of soft materials such as silks, satins, velvets and chiffon and are in subtle shades.

Skirts are long and full and worn over equally long petticoats. The tops of the bodice or dress are tight fitting with long, tight sleeves and a high neckline. Velvet jackets are sometimes worn over the dress, as in Armenia, where they are often made from a mulberry shade or dark blue velvet embroidered in gold and worn with a gold belt. Sleeves are often wide, reaching to the elbows, with the tight sleeves of the under-dress showing below. Long white veils fall from a round velvet pill box hat or from a silver band. These small hats are decorated with gold coins. The hair is dressed in two long plaits which fall down the front of the dress. These costumes are now worn chiefly by dancers and white or silver shoes with small heels are worn. Plate 37 illustrates one of the flowing costumes worn in Georgia.

Men's costumes present a complete contrast. They wear tight-fitting black trousers, worn with soft, pliable black leather, heel-less boots which are pulled on to fit rather like gloves. A white shirt is worn outside the trousers and is belted at the waist with a cord. The tight sleeves reach to the wrists and a tight band fits round the neck. A long Cossack style coat reaches to the knees and has narrow pockets for bullets on each side of the chest. The long sleeves of this coat completely cover the hands but they are usually rolled back to reveal the shirt. The coat and trousers are in black, brown, grey or white and the shirt black, white and sometimes red. A narrow belt is worn over the jacket and into this is fixed a dagger, often of great antiquity and which has been passed down from one generation to another. A black or grey astrakan hat is worn.

THE CENTRAL ASIAN REPUBLICS

UZBEKISTAN

The original inhabitants of the Asiatic republics were Moslems and the Islamic background is shown in the style of dress. Cotton is used extensively for clothing in Uzbekistan and the designs show a blending of colours in stripes of multi-coloured patterns (illustrated in Plate 38). As in many Asiatic countries, women wear trousers under their dresses or tunics. One of the most popular of the Uzbek women's costumes is the calf-length dress which has a turned-up collar and wide loose sleeves reaching to the wrists. The cotton trousers are white or in plain colours blending with the patterned dress and gathered into narrow bands. The black hair is dressed in several long, tiny plaits, the number marking the degree of beauty. A velvet, embroidered skull cap or 'tyubetevka' is worn both by men and women, with a tassel on festive occasions. Coloured shoes with low heels are worn.

The men wear loose fitting cotton coats called khalats. These are of knee length with coloured handkerchiefs tied round the waist, and are in various coloured stripes with long sleeves. A white shirt is worn under the coat and dark coloured trousers are tucked into black boots.

TURKMENISTAN

The famous Karakul sheep are bred in Turkmenistan and their grey, black or brown wool is used extensively in the making of costumes.

The women wear very colourful loose kaftans with long contrasting trousers which end in decorated bands. For special occasions fairly tight-fitting dresses in dark red or orange are worn. The seams of the front panel and the sides are outlined in white embroidery; the centre opening and neckline are also decorated. Trousers gathered into decorated bands are worn under the dress and are of the same colour and material. Plate 38 shows an elaborate costume which would be worn only on festive occasions. Cotton or heavy silk are used in the summer and fine wool in the winter.

The little round hat has a round dome ending in a metal point.

The hair is dressed in two long plaits and the shoes are soft, with slightly turned-up toes and small heels. A loosely fitting, three-quarter length coat is worn over the dress, in the same material and colour, although this would not be worn on informal occasions. The front edge, hem and the bottom of the sleeves are either embroidered or studded with metal discs.

Men wear tight-fitting black or brown trousers tucked into high black boots. A dark coloured, long-sleeved shirt in grey, brown or black is usual, although a white or red shirt is sometimes worn. Shirts have round necks with an opening on the right side, and are embroidered. The shirt is worn outside the trousers and a brightly coloured sash is worn with it.

A very large, sheepskin hat in white or brown is worn. Sometimes a loose, three-quarter length coat, similar to the Uzbek khalat, in two colour stripes is worn over the basic costume.

ROMANIA

The costumes and embroidery found in Romania reflect the Roman or Italian outlook in the use of colour and decoration, with beads, spangles, metal and silk threads, which have been developed in the Slavonic geometric patterns and love of embroidery. Parts of the costumes date from the time of the occupation by the Ottoman Empire.

The basic materials used for costumes are flax, hemp, wool and leather. The costumes underwent certain changes in the nineteenth century when cotton was imported on a large scale and was eventually produced in Romania. The growing of silk worms in the south-east region led to the introduction of silken tissues and thread which were used for veils and embroidery.

Of all the Balkan countries, the Romanian costumes are the richest in embroidery and design. Although there are variations from region to region, the embroidery retains the same characteristics, using designs in geometric form. Each region has a local pattern, the colours depending on the vegetable dyes available. Red is very popular in the north as the colour is obtained from the madder root. The basic colours are red, black, dark brown, blue, yellow and certain shades of green and violet. In the agricultural areas the colours tend to be brighter, but in the mountain districts darker hues predominate, such as dark red, and black with white. In all regions older people wear darker shades. In the southern Carpathians black and white embroidery is used extensively. The most widespread form of embroidery is the one thread type which demands very fine and careful needlework.

There are three main styles of women's costumes which are associated with various regions. The main features of regional costumes remain the same but colours, embroidery and other details change. In Oltenia, south of the Carpathians, and in Transylvania in the north, the main feature is the double apron. Over a white linen or cotton full smock or a skirt and blouse, two aprons are worn, one at the front and the other at the back. The aprons can have horizontal stripes of red, dark blue and white or, as found in the south, geometric designs in shades of yellow and white on a dark background. The aprons are also woven using metal thread and embroidered with beads.

In Wallachia, in the south, and towards Moldavia in the east, women wear a tight skirt or 'fota' woven in fine perpendicular stripes on a dark background. The stripes can be in any colour and around the hem is a band of embroidery or two broad red bands. In the region of Bacav the skirt has a black panel at the back and the sides and front woven in very bright narrow and broad stripes. The slim-line skirt is folded round the body and the front crossover portion is sometimes lifted and tucked into the braided waistband. The woman's skirt in Plate 39 shows the influence of the palace and the court styles which were once very popular. This black skirt is finely pleated and is worn over a woven panel. Both the skirt and the panel are made in heavy material and the embroidery gives an added weight to the costume. Under the skirt is a white petticoat which has an embroidered hem which sometimes shows below the skirt.

The skirt is worn over a white linen, hemp or cotton smock, which is often made in the old style of two pieces joined together and gathered with a cord round the neck and with sleeves added. This long-sleeved smock is embroidered in many colours, often with silver thread and beads.

In Banat, in the south-west, the more primitive form of costume is worn. Over the basic white smock is an apron but at the back there is a small oblong second apron called an 'opreg'. This little apron is woven in coloured patterns in wool, silk, cotton or metal threads. From the opreg hang long fringes of coloured wool called 'chite', which reach to the hem of the skirt. There are variations in the opregs, according to region, village and age.

The women's blouses are the most attractive features of the costumes throughout Romania. The upper part of the smock can form the blouse, or the skirts and blouses can be made separately. Sleeves are full and gathered into cuffs and the collarless neck is round. The blouse has bands of embroidery down the front, round the neck and cuffs, and down the sleeves as well as on the upper part of the sleeves.

Another interesting part of the costume is the long head veil, or 'marama'; originally made from hemp or linen, these were later replaced by fine cotton or silk (see Plate 39). The way of draping this veil indicates the age of the wearer. Married women wear the veil covering the head and crossed under the chin with one or both ends hanging down the back. Young girls wear the veil away from the face and draped down the back. In Oltenia the veils reach down to the level of the hem at the back.

In Banat the women wear a type of bonnet called a 'ccapsa' which is decorated with gold or silver thread, and in the Olt area straw hats decorated with flowers and ribbons are worn. With this costume laced-up ankle boots are worn. Coloured or plain headscarves, or scarves with a floral design, are worn in many regions.

Sheepskin jackets are popular in many regions and worn both by men and women, especially in winter. These are beautifully decorated and, again, the decoration varies according to the region: particularly noteworthy are those from Transylvania. White stockings are usually worn with the leather type sandal or 'opinci', although these are often now replaced by an ordinary black shoe.

Men's costumes can be divided into two styles, but with regional variations. The most popular form of dress, found in the south, east and north, consists of white trousers which are calf length and tucked into black boots or reach to the ankle and are worn with the opinci sandals. A white shirt with long sleeves loose at the wrist is worn like a tunic over the trousers and a broad leather belt or brightly woven waistband fastens round the waist (see Plate 39).

In some areas, however, the shirt is worn tucked into the trousers. In the Transylvania region in the north-west the costume reflects the Magyar influence, as shown in the full, white, loose trousers. Working clothes are simple and cut more loosely than those worn on more festive occasions. Summer trousers are usually made of cotton, but woollen trousers are worn in the winter. The long, tight fitting trousers, when worn with a tucked-in shirt, display a design in the front made with black or blue braid; this trouser decoration recalls the influence of the Ottoman Empire. Shirts are embroidered on the edges of the sleeves, hems, shoulders and upper sleeves and on the shirt front and collar. The colours and the amount of design used varies considerably from region to region. In some areas red is used only for older men and yellow for the young. In Maramures the shirt is short and the trousers loose and full: both are made from hemp. Characteristic of this region is the woven bag which hangs on the right side by means of a braided strap across the shoulder. The men also wear little straw or round felt hats which are decorated with braid and a feather on the side. A black sheepskin hat is very popular, being seen in many regions. The most spectacular hat comes from Bistrita-Nasavel and has a crown of peacock's feathers.

Also worn are coats, or a type of cloak, made in thick woollen material or drugget; these are either embroidered or trimmed with cord.

YUGOSLAVIA

Yugoslavia is comprised of six regions, each of which has its own particular character and costumes are highly individual.

The early Slav costume was predominantly white with a long smock for the woman, covered partly by an apron or sometimes an apron both back and front, worn with an over-dress or jacket.

The man had a similar smock or shirt with breeches and gaiters. This basic garb has changed only slightly and in some regions not at all. The Slavs are renowned for their skill in embroidery, used extensively in costume decoration. Designs are usually geometric or stem from Christian or Byzantine sources; red, together with black, predominates. Materials are wool, jute, flax and leather. Many costumes have coins hanging from chains worn round the neck and also fixed on to aprons, jackets and head-dresses. These coins represented the dowry of a daughter and in times of trouble were a very portable form of wealth.

1 **Iceland.** The woman on the left wears the more elaborate
costume used on ceremonial occasions.

2 **Lapland.** The 'cap of the four winds' is an older form of dress, not always worn today.

3 **Finland.** The inherent dignity of the Finns is reflected in their costumes.

4 **Norway.** The couple on the left wear a costume from east
Telemark; those on the right are from Voss.

5 **Sweden.** These costumes are all from the area around Stockholm.

6 **Denmark.** These costumes show various regional differences.

7 Netherlands. The couple both wear costumes from the village of Volendam.

8 France. These costumes are from the region of Provence.

9 **France.** The embroidery on these Breton costumes shows Celtic tradition.

10 **Belgium.** This couple wear costumes from Flanders, the
Flemish speaking region in the north.

11 German Democratic Republic. These attractive costumes are from southern regions.

12 **West Germany.** The woman wears a costume from the Black Forest, while the child comes from Hesse.

13 **West Germany.** This couple wear costumes typical of Bavaria.

14 Austria. A girl dressed in the dirndl costume pours brandy for
a climber in the Tyrol.

15 **Switzerland.** The herdsman is dressed in traditional costume: the woman is from the canton of Berne.

16 Italy. This couple from Aviano, in the north, hold handkerchiefs used in the dances of the region.

17 **Italy.** This boy and girl from Naples are about to dance the famous Tarantella.

18 England/Ireland. A traditional Morris dancer and a couple dressed for Irish dancing.

19 Scotland/Wales. The couple are dressed for Highland dancing. The Welsh woman wears traditional costume.

20 **Corsica/Malta.** The man on the left wears festival costume from Corsica; the couple are Maltese.

21 **Sardinia.** The woman wears the copricappa on her head; the man wears the birritta.

22 **Sicily.** This couple wear costumes from Piana degli Albanesi
which show Albanian influence.

23 **The Balearic Islands.** The woman on the left is from Ibiza.
The couple standing are from Majorca.

24 **Spain.** These two dancers from Andalusia are dressed in Flamenco costume.

25 **Spain.** This couple are from Aragon and wear the costume used to dance the Jota.

26 **Portugal.** This couple wear the costumes from Vianna do Castelo in the Minho region.

27 **Portugal/Madeira.** The couple are from the Algarve, Portugal.
The woman with the flowers is from Madeira.

28 The Canary Islands. The couple are both from Grand Canary and the little girl is from Tenerife.

29 **Czechoslovakia.** These dancers show the typical features of
costume from Bohemia.

30 Poland. This couple are from Lowicz which is famous for its
striped woollen material.

31 **Poland.** From Krakow, these are among the most popular of Polish costumes.

32 Hungary. The woman is from Géderlak, famous for its embroideries. The man is also from the central region.

33 Hungary. This couple wear costumes from the south-east of the country.

34 U.S.S.R. The woman on the left is from Latvia while the other woman wears one of the many Estonian costumes.

35 **U.S.S.R.** The woman on the right is from Byelorussia; the couple are Lithuanian.

36 **U.S.S.R.** The woman on the left wears the sarafan of the R.S.F.S.R. The couple are from the **Ukraine.**

37 **U.S.S.R.** The woman on the left is from Moldavia. The woman on the right is dressed in the costume from Georgia.

38 U.S.S.R. The woman on the left wears the distinctive costume of Uzbekistan. The woman on the right is from Turkmenistan.

39 **Romania.** This couple wear costumes from Vlasca near Bucharest. On their feet are opinci sandals.

40 **Yugoslavia.** This couple are from Sumadija in Serbia; a feature of their costume are their unusual shoes.

41 **Yugoslavia.** This couple are from Galicnik in western Macedonia, and are dressed for a festive occasion.

42 Bulgaria. These dancers from the Sop region of western Bulgaria perform the traditional 'hora' dances.

43 Albania. This couple wear two of the most striking costumes to be found in their country.

44 Greece. The man, an Evzone, wears the foustanella of the Greek guards. The woman wears the Amalia costume.

45 **Cyprus/Crete.** The woman on the right is from Cyprus. The couple are from the Greek island of Crete.

46 **Turkey.** These costumes from the south show the blending of colours and stripes so popular in this region.

47 Turkey. The woman wears the popular 'uç etek'. The man wears a festive costume from Balikesir in the west.

48 Iran. The man and the young girl are both from the nomadic Kashgai tribe which inhabits the south.

49 Morocco. The woman is a Berber from the Rif area of north Morocco. The man is a water vendor.

50 **Algeria.** The woman wears the loose fitting djellaba. The man is from one of the nomadic Tuareg tribes.

51 **Tunisia.** The woman wears the popular mellia while the man
is dressed in the summer djebba.

52 **Egypt.** The man wears a galabia, like the djellaba of north Africa. The woman wears a simple tunic.

53 The Lebanon. The most typical of the Lebanese costume is that of the Dabke shown here.

54 Ethiopia. This couple are from the Aderi tribe and come from Harar in the province of Hararghe.

55 **Saudi Arabia/Iraq.** The Kurdish man on the right is from Iraq. The child and her father are from Saudi Arabia.

56 **Israel.** This couple wear modern dance costumes evolved to
represent the new state of Israel.

57 Sri Lanka. This couple are dancers from Kandy, a famous place of pilgrimage for Buddhists.

58 India. This woman is dressed in the popular sari. The man is a
Sikh from north India.

59   **India.** Still mainly danced by girls, men now study and perform the Bharat Natyam dance.

60 Tibet/Afghanistan. The woman is from Utsang in Tibet. The
man wears typical workers' costume from Afghanistan.

61 **China.** The woman is a horserider from the Inner Mongolian
Autonomous Region. The man is a Yis from the south-west.

62 Thailand/Korea. These dancers of the classical Thai ballet are watched by a small Korean girl.

63 **Japan.** This couple are dressed for an important occasion such as a wedding.

64 The Philippines. The woman is dressed in the Patadiong style of costume. The man wears a Barong Tagalog.

65 Indonesia/Burma. The woman on the left is from Burma. The woman on the right is a Legong dancer from Bali.

66 New Zealand. These two Maoris are performing an action song. Their position means 'Welcome Friends'.

67 **Canada**. The woman is an Eskimo. The Kwakiutl Indian is dressed for a ceremonial dance.

68 U.S.A. This couple are dressed in the modern square dance costumes worn by demonstration groups.

69 **U.S.A.** The woman is a Sìoux Indian and the man belongs to one of the Woodland Tribes of the Great Lakes.

70 **Mexico.** The woman wears the embroidered huipil of Yucatan.
The man is a Huichol Indian from the west of Mexico.

71 **Mexico.** The woman is dressed in the china poblana costume. The man wears charro dress.

72 **Guatemala/Honduras.** The girl on the left is from Honduras.
The other two wear costumes for work in Guatemala.

73 Costa Rica. There are several variations of the woman's costume. The man wears typical clothes.

74 Panama. The woman wears the Pollera de Gala costume. The
man wears the country style fiesta costume known as Montuna.

75 **Cuba.** The woman's costume shows strong Spanish influence.
The man wears typical worker's dress.

76 Colombia/Venezuela. The man on the right is Venezuelan. The couple are from Colombia; he is a Llanero.

77 Brazil. The woman wears a costume showing European influence. The man is a cowboy from the sertao.

78 Peru/Bolivia. The woman on the right is an Aymara Indian from Bolivia. The couple are from Peru.

79 **Paraguay/Chile.** The woman wears the everyday costume of
Paraguay. The man is a cowboy from Chile.

80 **Argentina/Uruguay.** The man on the right is from Argentina.
The other is a horseman from Uruguay.

SLOVENIA

Here the women's full skirts reach to the calf and can be black, brown, red or gold. The large apron is of a contrasting colour and a full sleeved, high-necked white blouse is worn under a sleeveless bodice of the same material as the skirt. A brightly coloured floral shawl is draped across the front and covers the bodice. A decorated silver and gold chain fastened by a coloured bow is worn across one hip. There are several styles of hats; one of the most popular consists of a broad gold embroidered band, fastening at the back with a bow, and into which fine linen or cotton is gathered. White stockings and black, low-heeled shoes are worn.

Men wear black or brown breeches of leather or wool tucked into high black boots, or leather shorts worn over white under-trousers tucked into green, knee-high gaiters. A sleeveless black, brown or green waistcoat is fastened up the front with silver buttons. The long-sleeved shirt is white with cuffs. Black felt hats with either large or small brims are worn.

CROATIA

This is the one region in Yugoslavia which has a diversity of costumes. Those on the Hungarian borders have full, white, short skirts decorated with open-work embroidery, colourful blouses with white frilled necks, floral patterned shawls and aprons, striped stockings and decorated shoes. The men wear the Hungarian style, white linen, full trousers, with a white shirt worn outside under a decorated sleeveless waistcoat. Black boots are worn.

On the Dalmatian coast the Italian influence is seen in the long pleated skirts, either in white or dark colours, which are worn with black or coloured aprons. Jackets have long sleeves and the white folded head-dresses are based on the Italian 'tovaglia'.

In Krk, short black skirts with red, yellow and blue coloured borders are worn with low-cut sleeveless bodices in red or black, coloured aprons and white, full-sleeved blouses. Red or white stockings are worn with coloured shoes. A white, folded tovaglia is worn with two ends falling down the back or golden ribbons are draped on the head. Men wear long, black, baggy trousers reaching to the ankles, black sleeveless waistcoats or black jackets. Shirts are white with full sleeves, socks are white and black, and silver-buckled shoes are worn. On the head is a fisherman's black woollen type hat.

One of the most interesting costumes found in Croatia has an apron with an extended bib with both sections covered with coins. This is worn over a long-sleeved smock and a red, sleeveless coat. Decorated white stockings are worn with leather sandals, and red pill box hats, plain or covered with coins, have white veils. The man's costume which accompanies this style has wide, dark blue, baggy trousers fastened into red decorated gaiters. A broad sash is sometimes worn with a studded leather belt and pistol. Plain, striped or patterned waistcoats, with or without sleeves and fastening on the side, are worn over white, long-sleeved shirts. A short bolero type of jacket, decorated with gold or coloured braid, is worn over the waistcoat. A round hat, adapted from the Turkish fez and which sometimes has a black fringed tassel, is worn. Soft leather slippers are usual.

BOSNIA-HERCEGOVINA

The costumes from this region are less elaborate. A feature of the women's dress is the short sleeveless waistcoat which ends several inches above the waist and is known as a 'zubun'. In Bosnia the zubun is black, embroidered in gold, and is worn over the long, white smock or dress which has long loose sleeves. Round the waist a braided coloured belt is fastened with a large silver clasp. Dark stockings and traditional leather sandals are worn. Hats are small pill box shapes or are of draped red and white linen, as in the Italian-style tovaglia.

In Hercegovina the zubun is in pastel shades or in red, decorated with gold embroidery. An apron in horizontal stripes or a floral pattern woven in a striped design, is worn over a white dress. The edge of the apron has a deep woollen fringe. Embroidery is multicoloured, but with red as the predominant colour. In Bosnia the predominant colours are black and red. A loose-fitting, three-quarter length, sleeveless jacket in red or white is very popular.

In Bosnia, men wear loose, long, white linen trousers or brown or white baggy trousers which taper to fit tightly round the calf and lower leg. Black or blue sleeveless waistcoats are worn with broad sashes or belts. White shirts have long sleeves and a dark red turban is wound round the head. Dark stockings and leather sandals complete the costume.

Men in Hercegovina wear full, dark blue, baggy trousers which are gathered below the knees. A black patterned sock reaches only to the calf leaving a gap between the trousers and the socks. Heavily embroidered gold waistcoats are worn under jackets and wide, multi-coloured or dark red sashes hold several daggers.

MONTENEGRO

Here the costumes are very elegant, the women's red zubun being encrusted with gold floral embroidery and having long or short sleeves. The high-necked, white dress has a silver belt, which is decorated, and a white three-quarter length sleeveless jacket embroidered in gold is worn. To complete the costume there are white stockings, leather sandals and a little black, round pill box hat.

Men wear dark blue, full trousers gathered into a band below the knees. White stockings have decorated bands at the ankles. Cross-over waistcoats in red, purple and crimson are decorated with braid, over which a very ornamental white or blue knee-length coat is worn. This coat has long sleeves with a second loose sleeve hanging down the back.

SERBIA

Like the region, the costumes of Serbia vary considerably. Those from Leskovac have black sleeveless bodices and skirts. Gold braid decorates the low, round front of the bodice as well as the hem of the skirt. The white under-dress has a high neckline with wide loose sleeves embroidered with open-work. The dress hangs well down below the skirt hem and has a border of lace. A long white scarf is draped round the head and neck. Coloured patterned socks and leather sandals with slightly turned-up toes are worn.

In Sumadija, the skirt is pleated and has a horizontal striped pattern of blues, yellow and black. A red apron in stripes and geometrical patterns is worn with a red bodice and white blouse. Sometimes the pleated skirt is folded and caught at the back to reveal the under-dress. Plate 40 illustrates a couple dressed in a costume from Sumadija.

White skirts are worn with perpendicular or horizontal striped aprons and a three-quarter length sleeveless jacket. Embroidery can be simple or ornate with a predominance of geometric designs rather than floral ones. Red, dark blue, yellow, black and orange are used extensively. Decorated socks and sandals with very turned-up toes are worn.

The men have rather baggy trousers tucked into brightly patterned socks reaching to just below the knees. Short waistcoats and jackets, made in dark brown woollen material, are worn. Wide belts of leather with handsome silver clasps are also worn. The white linen shirts have loose sleeves. Round black sheepskin hats and sandals with turned-up toes complete the costumes.

MACEDONIA

The basic dress of the women is a long, white linen smock with loose or gathered sleeves ending in cuffs. A geometrical design is embroidered in black or red around the hem, sleeves and neck and this embroidery can vary from the very elaborate to the simple, according to the occasion. A three-quarter length white jacket, which can have either long sleeves or be sleeveless, is elaborately decorated with embroidery and braid. The Macedonian costumes are the most heavily decorated of the Yugoslavian dress, with a blending of reds, orange, yellow and black in both the embroidery and the weaving. The rather heavy red woven aprons end in a deep woollen fringe and across the front there is a chain with silver coins: similar chains are worn round the neck. Coins are sometimes used on the aprons as part of a design. A large belt fastened with an elaborate silver buckle is worn round the waist. Stockings are knitted in red, white and black patterns and are worn with soft leather sandals. The head-dress consists of a white cotton scarf or veil, draped over the head and falling down the back; the edge is often embroidered with silver coins fixed at the front. An elaborate version of this costume for a festive occasion is shown in Plate 41.

In eastern Macedonia men wear a white shirt with sleeves reaching to the elbows. A gathered skirt reaches to just above the knees and a broad decorated belt is worn. Under the skirt, white linen or cotton trousers are tucked into knee-high socks. Patterns using dark coloured wools such as deep plum, black or dark blue with a red star in a diamond design are displayed on these socks, which are worn with the traditional leather sandals. A sleeveless waistcoat, braided round the edges and in dark colours, is favoured. A round black sheepskin hat or a draped and knotted white turban is worn. In the west, in the region of Galicnik, white or cream, tight-fitting woollen trousers replace the skirts. The trouser seams, front and ankles have bands of black braid as decoration (see Plate 41). Short or long-sleeved, dark maroon waistcoats are worn with a black or brown short-sleeved over-jacket. A white shirt, leather sandals and a very small flat, round hat is worn.

BULGARIA

Although the influence of Islam is evident in the music, dances and costumes of Bulgaria, the designs in embroidery, weaving and folk art remain Slavonic. The main materials used were hemp, flax, cotton, wool and goat hair, with locally produced silk used only for special costume decorations and embroidery.

Embroidery followed the traditional patterns of triangles, squares and diamonds and geometric forms were often used in the abstract portrayal of stars, plants, animals and human figures. There was a great variation of motifs and colours. Each group of costumes had variants according to the district, from which it was possible to identify region, village and even household.

Women's costumes are divided into four main styles which are associated with different regions. In the north the costume consists of the basic Slav long white smock with long sleeves and a high neckline. Over the smock is worn a type of knee-length skirt or apron which fits round the body and fastens at the waist with an opening down the front; a second apron is worn over the skirt to hide the gap. A loose sleeveless jacket is also worn. There are many variations of this basic costume and the calf-length hem of the smock, the sleeves and the neck opening are all embroidered in different designs, again varying according to the region. Sleeves can be loose or gathered into cuffs. The gathered or finely pleated over-skirt or apron is in red, black and orange perpendicular stripes whilst the smaller apron has a woven horizontal striped pattern. The jacket can also be striped or plain, a specially embroidered sleeveless jacket being worn by a bride on her wedding day. Knitted socks in various colours are worn with the Balkan-type leather sandal.

A costume characteristic of the central part of Bulgaria and which has now spread to other parts of the country is the 'sukman', a type of tunic or over-dress. This can have long sleeves although the more popular version is sleeveless. It is made in black, blue or red wool for the winter and cotton is used in the summer. The sukman can be decorated or embroidered in various different ways and is worn over the basic white smock. Ornamental leather belts with elaborate silver buckles are very popular. A short apron is often worn with this costume, together with a short- or long-sleeved jacket. Young girls wear a simple flowered head-dress or headscarf and married women have scarves completely covering the hair. Stockings can be white, black or white with a pattern of stripes and are worn with leather sandals.

A costume found in the south and south-west has a type of coat or over-dress called a 'saya'. This can have either long or short sleeves, is open down the front and again is worn over the basic white smock. The saya is made of black or blue woollen material, replaced in the summer by brightly striped cotton, although the older women wear darker cotton colours. The neck, sleeves and hem of the woollen sayas are often decorated with embroidery, appliqué, lace or finely braided patterns.

A large apron covers the central opening and there is a deep waistband or belt. Aprons made of a check material are found in the south; colours vary according to age and marital status. The older women choose darker colours. A long headscarf in a printed design is folded into a triangle and the ends tied at the back of the head; this replaces the white scarf of former years.

Knitted stockings are often made on five needles. Formerly thick felt slippers with embroidered uppers were worn for special occasions, but these have now been replaced by leather sandals. Silver bracelets, necklaces, ear-rings, and coins all appear in most regions on festive occasions.

In the south the older style of costume is still found. This consists of a large apron worn over the smock and is worn mostly during the summer months; it can be combined with a saya and a jacket. On the Yugoslav border the aprons have diamond patterns of black and white on an orange-red background. A similar coloured sleeveless jacket is worn tucked under the apron. Braided belts, which are very popular in Bulgaria, are worn with this costume, with a white scarf draped round the face. White or black stockings and the usual leather sandals are worn.

Men's costumes have two main styles. The older style, which was first favoured in the north-east and then became popular in other regions, has white woollen, tight-fitting trousers reaching to the ankles. The trousers are decorated with black cord which not only reinforces the seams, but makes shaped patterns on the front. A white, long-sleeved shirt is worn under a sleeveless white or black jacket. In some regions a white, knee-length coat is worn, with or without sleeves. A patterned, chequered or striped waistband, or 'Tukanitsa', is worn either over the long coat or under the short jacket. For a young man this is in dark red or blue and the older men wear black or a dark colour. White socks and leather sandals are usual, with a round black sheepskin hat. When wearing the 'white' costume there is a variety of choice in the jacket preferred.

Plate 42 shows a couple from the Sop region of western Bulgaria dancing the traditional 'horas'. The man is dressed in the 'white' costume.

The alternative costume worn by the men replaces the 'white' costume and is more comfortable to wear. It consists of trousers which are full and baggy at the top and are made in black, brown and occasionally blue woollen material. Black braid decorates the trousers in the same pattern as in the 'white' costume. Different types of long-sleeved shirts are worn, ranging from plain white to embroidery on white or made in fine red and black stripes. A black sleeveless waistcoat is worn over the shirt and in winter or on festive occasions a sleeved jacket is worn, either inside or out of the waistband. Round the lower leg and over the trousers long strips of woollen or flaxen cloth are wrapped spirally. Alternatively, thick white knitted socks and long felt boots or leather sandals are worn. The men's costume is completed by black sheepskin hats.

ALBANIA

The costumes of Albania are very individual although they show the influence of other countries in design. Wool, woven at home, was obtained from the mountain sheep and the more affluent costumes would be decorated with elaborate embroideries with braids of gold and silver thread and coloured silks.

Women's costumes are in two styles, those with trousers and those with skirts, but both have numerous variations. The trousers can be very full and gathered in at the ankles and the colours used are dark maroon, shades of pink, gold and many other colours in cotton or satin. With them are worn long tight-fitting jackets or bodices made in dark coloured materials, and covered with silver embroidery or gold braid. A high, round-necked white blouse has wide loose sleeves with a ribbon or braid tied round the arms just above the elbows. A sash or silver belt is worn round the waist. There are heel-less slippers with embroidered toes or plaited leather sandals. A round pill box hat is worn at the back of the head or a coloured scarf with a pointed end which is tied at the back. The head-dress shown in Plate 43 consists of a veil draped over a white fez.

The men's costumes are also in two styles, those with trousers or, alternatively, a pleated skirt, or foustanella. The Ghegs wear white or black woollen trousers which fit tightly to the ankles; the seams are decorated with black braid. A white shirt with long sleeves, either loose or with cuffs is worn under a white and braided sleeveless waistcoat. Waistcoats vary between the villages. Plate 43 shows a version of this costume. In Kukes, in the north-east, a rust red waistcoat with dark blue facings, is worn with a broad striped sash, rust coloured socks and black leather sandals. In the south-east black baggy trousers are tucked into white felt gaiters and tied under the knees with black cord. The costume is completed with a red sash and a black jacket decorated with gold braid. Loose sleeves hang down the back. The unusual white shirt which is worn has a small round collar, and wide loose sleeves reaching to the elbows, under which long tight sleeves reach to the wrists. Shoes are black and edged with red. The most popular form of hat is the white felt fez.

The pleated white linen skirt, or foustanella, is less full than those worn in Greece and reaches to the knees. Long white woollen tight trousers are worn underneath this skirt. A plain white woollen sleeveless waistcoat edged with black braid is worn with a white, wide-sleeved shirt and a black fringed coloured sash. Over this is a black jacket with loose hanging sleeves. The white shirt has sleeves gathered into cuffs, and black or light brown leather sandals with large black pom poms are worn. A white fez or a black forage-cap type of hat are the alternative headgear.

The colours used throughout Albania are: basic black, white and a particular shade of rust red together with a range of pastel colours. Designs are usually geometric with zig zags, squares, triangles and an occasional floral pattern.

GREECE

Nearly half of the present day population of Greece lives in rural areas. The people tend sheep and goats and the wool, spun and woven in the homes, is used for their costumes. In the Macedonia areas mulberry trees flourish and silk is produced. Flax is also grown and the linen used extensively in the making of costumes.

The costumes in the north-east have much in common with those of Bulgaria. Over a basic white smock or under-dress, a horizontal striped apron is worn, or a dark blue or black tunic dress, or sukman, which has the embroidered edge of the smock showing below the hem. With these costumes is worn a long-sleeved jacket which fits into the waist and is decorated very simply with gold thread and fine braid. Silver belts, knitted socks, soft leather sandals and chains with coins worn across the jacket front, are found in this area. Dark or patterned headscarves and Greek berets with long black tassels are worn.

In the Epirus region the basic white smock or under-dress has wide sleeves which have ribbons or braid tied round the arms just above the elbows.

Plain aprons, worn on the hips rather than round the waist, are found in Pogoni, whilst patterned or striped aprons are worn in other areas. Long or short jackets, with or without sleeves, are also popular. White or gaily patterned knitted stockings are worn with simple black shoes or leather sandals with black pom poms on the toes. Silk or linen headscarves are either draped round the face or worn so that they fall down the back.

It is in the central and southern region that the very distinctive Greek style is seen. Here the long skirts echo the flowing robes of their ancestors and in these regions there is a wide range of colours and materials: silk, cotton or linen is often used. Colours are subtle shades of blue, red, green and yellow used in conjunction with gold and silver thread embroidery or fine braid. An apron is sometimes worn over these long skirts.

Plate 44 shows a woman dressed in the Amalia costume. This costume was specially created and named after Queen Amalia and has become part of the country's tradition. The ankle length skirt can be in a variety of colours, pastel shades being very popular. The gold embroidered jacket, which is worn over a blouse, can be simpler than the one that is shown. The red cap has a long silk tassel.

In Perahora a white linen, long-sleeved dress, with a deep border of black and orange embroidery round the hem and the sleeves, is worn. The short apron has a black fringed edge and is also embroidered in black. A black hip length coat with half sleeves is worn and the tight fitting black beret cap has two long tassels draped down the left side. White stockings and backless embroidered shoes are worn, while numerous gold coins hang from the neck.

Long-sleeved, tight fitting jackets worn over a blouse or dress are found in many regions. Colours and styles vary according to the region and sometimes they are made of velvet or wool and braided or embroidered in gold thread or silk. They can be fastened at the waist, forming a type of bodice, or worn loose.

Costumes from Attiki, Trikeri and Karagouna, resemble those of ancient Greece in style. A long, ankle-length, full skirt has an over-dress or tunic reaching to the thighs or knees; it is either in white or a contrasting shade and is worn with a belt.

Men's costumes can be divided into two styles, those based on the baggy or long trousers and those on the white skirt or foustanella. The costumes are fairly simple and usually of dark colours which highlight the striking dresses of the women. Each region has a characteristic feature: in Thrace the men wear dark woollen trousers which are cut in a special way and called 'poutouri'. It was from these trousers that the name of the costume—the Poutouria—was derived.

In Macedonia they wear the 'Panovraki', or long under-trousers, which are covered by a skirt. These trousers are also found in other regions and are made in white cotton or wool and tucked into leggings or brightly coloured knitted socks. The baggy trousers or 'vraka' are very popular on the islands.

In the Peloponnese, Attica and other parts of the Greek mainland, the characteristic garment is the white 'foustanella' (see Plate 44). First introduced into Greece by Albanian warriors it was adopted by the Greek soldiers as it gave freedom of movement. Made from panels of white linen, the garment was covered with fat to make it rain-proof and turned the material into an off-white or grey colour. The foustanella is worn mainly on Sundays as trousers are worn as a working dress.

Short bolero style waistcoats, or gileki, are worn and these are plain for work and decorated with braid and embroidery for formal or festive wear. These waistcoats are usually sleeveless, but in some regions, as in the southern Peloponnese, they have loose sleeves which hang from the shoulders. Sleeves of shirts are open or gathered into cuffs. Coloured shirts are used for work, but white is the formal colour. Broad sashes are tied round the waist; in Macedonia a black sash is worn by older men and dark red by the younger men. A bridegroom will have a belt of coins round his sash.

Shoes with pom poms ('tsarouhia') or boots are the most usual form of footwear. Black or black and white socks are exchanged for more brightly coloured ones on holiday occasions.

Round caps or hats are made from lambswool, velvet, felt and are often in black. A type of fez with a long tassel is also very popular.

CRETE

The costumes of Crete denote past influences and the Cretans are a proud and defiant race although they still retain the characteristic friendliness of the Greeks. The men's costumes portray their background very strongly, with white Minoan boots ('stivalia'), Turkish baggy trousers ('vraka') and rather severely cut jackets. Usually a dagger is thrust through a purple sash or 'zounari' which is eight metres long. The illustration in Plate 45 shows a black costume, but a similar style is made in dark blue wool with a sleeveless waistcoat, or gileki, cut with a diagonal fastening. The waistcoat is red and the shirt white.

The women's costume has full white trousers worn under a white cotton dress. Over this is worn an apron with an embroidered hem and a tight fitting jacket. A red sash is tied around the waist with the long end falling to one side. A red hat of draped cotton and black leather shoes are worn. Plate 45 shows this costume.

CYPRUS

Costumes are now only seen in Cyprus on festive occasions. They are made of wool, silk, cotton and a blend of silk and cotton called 'itare'. Silk worms are bred on the island and all the materials are woven in the homes; wool comes from the fat tailed Cypriot sheep.

Two styles of dress are popular: the Karpasitiko costume has a white, long-sleeved dress which is calf length with a high round neck. Under the dress are worn full white trousers which can be embroidered or plain. A tight fitting, long coat has loose sleeves and turned-back cuffs, which are decorated. The front of the coat is low cut and shows the dress. The coat can be made from a range of materials and colours. A white or coloured handkerchief is worn, draped or folded, on the head. This handkerchief can be embroidered or have a lace edging; geometrical designs and patterns are very popular.

The other form of dress is a black velvet, long-sleeved jacket worn with a long silk or cotton skirt, shown in Plate 45. The skirt can be in plain colours or white, stripes—which are very popular—or checks. The bodice is decorated with gold or coloured braid. A red fez or white handkerchief are often worn on the head. Black low heeled shoes are worn with both costumes.

The men's costumes have full, baggy black trousers or 'vraka' tucked into black boots. A black sash is tied round the waist and a black embroidered or patterned sleeveless waistcoat is worn over a white, long-sleeved shirt. A little round black cap is worn on the back of the head.

The Turkish population, on festive occasions, wear the costumes seen on the mainland. Blue is a popular colour. The red fez, draped turbans and loose jackets are still worn for work.

TURKEY

A third of Turkey's population lives in the towns and cities and the remainder in rural communities, some of which are very remote. Folk customs are still observed and costumes maintained, as is evident at festivals or other celebrations. The costume materials are woven in the homes and the actions of weaving are often demonstrated in many of the folk dances. Materials are light in weight, mostly in cotton and silk with floral or striped patterns. Embroidery is not used extensively although it may be found occasionally on jackets and trousers.

Women's costumes are most decorative with the various articles of dress blending colours together, thus making the use of embroidery unnecessary. Shades of red are frequently incorporated into the costumes as this is regarded as a protection against malign influences. Henna is also used for this purpose and parts of the body are stained with it.

The basic costume has changed very little over the centuries and there is little variation between the regions. Very full and baggy trousers called 'Salvar' or shalvar, are worn by women in most areas (see Plates 46 and 47). In the eastern region of Elazig they are worn with long-sleeved white blouses and sleeveless waistcoats. The waistcoats are usually in the same material and colour as the trousers. Round the waist is worn a coloured and fringed sash. The waistcoat is often replaced by a long-sleeved jacket of waist length and this can be in a similar or a contrasting colour. Those for special occasions are decorated with gold thread or braid on the cuffs, the edges and the back. Occasionally the side seams and the front of the trousers are similarly decorated.

A very popular costume found in many regions is a long-sleeved, high-necked jacket or coat which reaches to the calf. The skirt section of the jacket is in three panels, with one at the back and two at the front, and this garment is known as 'üç etek'. This is illustrated in Plate 47. For working or dancing one of the front panels can be lifted and tucked into the belt or sash. Alternatively, both front panels can be folded back and fastened at the rear, a style which is found in the south. In the north, in the region of Corum, the front panels are crossed over, forming a type of apron. The material of these jackets is mainly woven in perpendicular stripes and in a variety of colours and the baggy salvar in a plain contrasting shade.

Another type of costume worn a great deal is based on a coloured, long-sleeved dress reaching to the calf or ankle with the conventional trousers underneath, but there are many variations of this costume. In Gaziantep, in the south near the Syrian border, the skirt only reaches to the thigh and is white in colour. It is worn with a black, floral patterned short jacket. In Irabazon, a northern region on the Black Sea, part of the skirt hem is lifted up and tucked into a belt.

Religion and custom decreed that no man or woman should allow any hair to be seen, so both sexes wore a form of head-dress. In all the costumes the only part of the body exposed were the hands. Until recently women covered their faces with veils, or draped scarves. The most popular form of head-dress is the round fez or pill box shaped hat with a veil or silk scarf draped over it. The ends of the scarf either hang down the back or fasten under the chin. Often the fez is decorated with gold and silver coins with chains across the forehead. When the fez is not worn, a long scarf is tied in various ways over the head.

Soft leather type sandals called yemeni are mostly worn and these can have slightly turned-up toes (see Plate 46). In the southern region these shoes are usually red. The shoes illustrated in Plate 47 are more modern and would not be used for working.

There are three different styles of trousers for the men. The full baggy salvar, which is similar to those of the women are usually in black or various shades of blue (see Plate 46); a brown or black trouser called a 'zivka' is also very common and this is tight-fitting below the knees, but has several extra folds in the upper part of the garment, especially at the back. The other form of trouser is based on the full salvar, but ends at the knees and the lower part of the legs are covered by gaiters as is shown in Plate 47. High-necked, white, long-sleeved shirts are usually worn with sleeveless waistcoats or short jackets. The jackets, called cepken, are sometimes embroidered or decorated with braid. Striped shirts are

189

worn in some areas. A red felt fez is a popular form of head-dress around which is tied a turban. In some regions just the turban is worn and can be in one colour or multi-coloured. A coloured scarf is sometimes tied and knotted round the head. Along the Black Sea coast a covering called a baslik is worn; this consists of a long, black scarf rolled and knotted on the head like a turban, but the two ends hang on either side like ears. Soft leather yemeni in black or brown are worn, but in the east and on the Black Sea coast soft black calf boots are more usual. A very broad striped sash or waist band is worn, sometimes with a broad leather belt over the top. Into this belt various weapons are fixed.

A very unusual costume comes from Bursa where the men dance the famous kiliç kalkan, or sword and shield dance, dressed in early Ottoman military costumes. Dark blue trousers rather like shorts, a striped orange shirt and a short blue jacket with hanging sleeves are worn. A deep waistband and a striped turban wrapped round the fez completes the costume. The soft leather shoes have a criss-cross lacing over white knee-length stockings.

IRAN

There are many ethnic groups living in Iran, each having its own costumes, which are simple in design and loosely cut to suit the warm climate. Islamic laws require women to be veiled, but this is not strictly adhered to in the larger towns and cities. In the more remote villages, however, the women still wear the enveloping cloak called a 'chador'. This is worn over the head and draped round the body and pulled across the face when necessary. In the south, along the Persian Gulf, and in some other areas a black face mask is worn.

Cotton and flax are mainly used for costumes, being grown in the coastal areas round the Caspian sea. In the fertile valleys mulberry trees flourish and silk is produced which is used in the making of costumes worn on special occasions. In the city of Yadz, a silk tissue known as Yasdi is made.

The women's costumes are very colourful and the Iranians have a particular love of flowers, roses and carnations being grown extensively in some regions. Trousers are worn with most costumes and have a straight line.

The basic costume consists of a loose tunic with long sleeves worn over a very full skirt and trousers. These tunics vary in colour, length and design. In Gilan, a region in the north-west, a deep waistband in red and yellow stripes is worn over a red, hip length tunic. The skirt is white with bands of red, blue, green and black round the hem. Worn with this costume are red trousers. From Luristan, near Teheran, the loose knee-length tunic is worn with matching trousers and no skirt. In the southern region of Bandar Abbas, on the Persian Gulf, the loose red or blue tunic reaches to the ankles. Over the tunic, a little striped cotton, sleeveless jacket is worn. A long headscarf passes round the neck, across the back and ties in the front round the waist. On the Pakistan border, the loose tunic has bands of coloured braid from the high, round neck down to the hem. The decoration varies according to the village. The trousers and tunic hem can also have bands of braid. The Kashgai women wear a loose, full, calf or knee-length tunic which is open at the side seams nearly to the waist. Under this is worn a full, ankle-length skirt and trousers. The head and hair are always covered, either by a round, tight-fitting cap, embroidered with beads or coins, over which is a long scarf, passing under the chin: a turban can replace the hat, but most common is a very long, white or coloured scarf, draped round the head, with the older women wearing black or darker colours. Plate 48 shows a young girl wearing this costume. Embroidered shoes with slightly turned-up toes and small heels are worn for special occasions, otherwise canvas or soft leather boots are the usual footwear.

The men wear full, white, baggy shalvar trousers over which is a white shirt; the sleeves and edges of the shirt are often edged with bands of red. A coloured waistcoat is worn and a white or yellow turban is worn on the head.

Another costume is the kaftan, reaching to the ankles with a broad coloured sash tied round the waist. The Kashgai men wear a blue striped, calf-length coat which has loose sleeves and over which is worn a wide sash. The side of the coat is open, showing blue or dark coloured trousers. This costume is shown in Plate 48. An ankle boot of soft leather is worn and a felt cap with turned-up side wings.

The Kurds maintain their tribal dress with great pride. The men wear short, thigh-length jackets, fastened to the neck or open down the front. Blue with a very fine blue stripe is a popular choice of colour or a blue material woven in small squares to give a quilted look. Kurdish men wear white shirts with very long sleeves which are wrapped round the jacket cuffs or allowed to hang down.

The white or coloured turbans are fringed and tied in such a way that the fringe falls across the face, acting as a 'fly whisk'. Turbans are worn in many regions and are sometimes wound round a small type of fez with a corrugated pattern. Round felt skull caps and hats are also worn. Shoes and sandals are made in canvas or lightweight soft leather.

MOROCCO

The mountainous terrain of Morocco has restricted communication and there is a marked contrast in the clothes worn in the towns and the villages and between the Arabs and the Berbers.

The women in the cities wear the loose-fitting djellaba in white, grey or blue made in cotton or gaberdine. This garment reaches to the ankles and has a hood attached. Across the face a short black or white cotton veil is fastened; this practice is not always followed by the younger girls, however. An enveloping cloak, the haik, is also worn, often over European clothes. The haik is made in white or black cotton, wool or a mixture of cotton and silk. The draping of this cloak varies in different areas.

In Morocco the kaftan is very popular and at one time worn by both men and women; now it is essentially a woman's garment. It is a long garment with wide and loose sleeves, fastened in the front with a row of small buttons which are usually made of silk braid. The kaftan is worn over an under-garment of light material called a 'quich' and this covers the loose, full trousers, or seroval, which reach to just below the knee.

The kaftan is worn indoors, but is covered by a striped djellaba or white haik outdoors. The old style of very elaborate kaftans in heavy brocade are now only worn by brides. Women wear backless babouche slippers of Moroccan leather embroidered and decorated in a variety of designs.

Very colourful and unusual are the Berber costumes found in the south and the mountain ranges. A loose tunic dress, which acts as the basic garment, can have draped over it either a haik or a long piece of material called an 'izar'. The izar is not unlike the Tunisian 'mellia'; the material is joined at the sides and the wearer fastens the back section to the front by pulling it over the shoulders and fixing it with fibula pins. The colour of the material depends upon the locality.

In Goulimine the izar is blue and worn over a black tunic. The Tiznit women wear a black izar over a white tunic with enormous fibula pins. The Ait Hadidou tribe of the High Atlas wear a white one held at the waist with a woollen belt decorated with coloured pom-poms.

The Tissint women south of Agadir dress entirely in black or indigo blue and also have coloured woven belts. Very fine cotton voile is draped round the waist by several groups, rather like an over-skirt, and the basic tunic is in a floral pattern. In the winter a long piece of woollen material, woven by the women themselves and called an 'hiyyak' or hendira, is worn like a cloak. This material is often woven in stripes and each tribe has a different pattern as well as a way of wearing it. Plate 49 shows the hiyyak worn by a Berber woman from the Rif area of north Morocco.

There are numerous forms of head-dresses, usually with a loose head covering which can be drawn across the face when required. The Berber women tend to cover their faces only in the towns or if they think they are being observed or photographed. Headwear ranges from simple straw hats to long white or black fringed scarves knotted at the back. In parts of the south a coloured scarf is tied round a little brocade cap, with a silver band of coins which cover the forehead.

The women near Telovet in the south wear skeins of twisted coloured wool, kept in place by silver clips and ornaments. The hair is often plaited and worn on the top of the head and married women or widows use henna as a hair dye. Hand-made silver jewellery is worn by most Berber women and this usually represents the wealth of the family. The fibula pins are quite large and beautifully worked and are studded with stones. Very long and elaborate chains hang across the chest from each pin. Large amber and coloured beads, the size of eggs, are also much prized. Jewellery is worn as for special occasions such as weddings.

Men also wear the hooded djellaba, made in either cotton or wool, according to the season, and in a variety of colours, although white is the most popular. The djellaba is worn over European dress or an under shirt with or without sleeves. The garment is made with two slits at the sides, which allows the hands access to the leather satchel or bag which hangs from a woollen cord across one shoulder. This bag is sometimes worn outside the djellaba.

In the north, striped djellabas are worn for special occasions and are made in heavy silk. In the south, the djellaba is replaced by a long loose shirt of blue cotton and is known as a 'derraa'. On the front there is a big pocket which is embroidered with a different design according to the Saharan region. With this costume the men wear a long white or blue scarf, called a 'shesh', around the head and neck as a protection against the sun or sandstorms. The men of the Rif mountains wear short djellabas with a wide leather belt round the waist.

In the famous market square of Jemaa el Fna in Marrakesh, it is possible to see a whole range of unusual costumes worn by various traders and entertainers. In Plate 49 the man wears a costume which denotes his specific trade, that of water vendor. The Gnaouas entertain the crowds by dancing, and wear calf-length, long-sleeved white shirts which are belted at the waist. Loose, knee-length trousers are worn and round black hats are decorated with white cowrie shells and beads. Acrobats, who are dressed in coloured baggy trousers and white shirts, belong to the brotherhood of Sidi Ahmed ou Moussa, south of the Anti Atlas mountains.

ALGERIA

The most popular form of dress in Algeria is the long cotton or gaberdine hooded djellaba in white, grey or blue, which is worn with a short veil across the face; this is illustrated in Plate 50. Alternatively, there is a large enveloping cloak, or haik, in white or black cotton or wool, according to the season of the year. It is draped round the body, pulled over the head and can be drawn across the face. In the cities, European clothes are often worn under the haik. Kaftans are worn indoors or under the djellaba or haik when outdoors.

Away from the capital, the costumes are based on the style known as 'Mellia'. This is a long length of material draped round the body and fastened on the shoulders with two fibula pins. A belt or sash is tied round the waist, giving a blouse effect to the upper part of the garment. The fibula pins vary in size, some are very large and some are joined across the chest by silver chains; all are beautifully decorated. On festive occasions women from the mountain areas wear belts made of silver discs.

An under-dress of a contrasting colour or fine stripes will have a mellia draped over it and this is also a style favoured by the Berber mountain women. Many of the Berber tribes spend a nomadic existence and each tribe has a slightly different style of dress but they all share a love of colour, using blues, pinks, dark reds and purple.

Another style of dress is an ankle-length, loose cotton under-tunic which has a short mellia draped over it without a belt or sash. This can be in the same colour, in contrasting colours or floral patterns and can be edged with gold or coloured braid.

In the mountain regions during the winter months or at night in the desert a woollen or thick goat hair cape is tied round the shoulders. This is known as a hiyyak or hendira and it is also a protection against the sirocco winds and the sudden sand storms.

On festive occasions, the women of Kabylia, in the north, wear a white costume with an elaborately designed silver belt. On their heads they wear a diadem hung with silver discs and pendants set with coral and enamel, silver ornaments and jewellery being much prized. Berber women usually have a chain hung with various charms including the Hand of Fatma and square amulets. Little leather purses containing verses from the Koran are fastened on to a cord and they are worn round the neck.

Head-dresses vary from region to region and also among the tribes. Headscarves are tied and knotted in numerous ways round the head like turbans, and under the turban there is sometimes a piece of material which protects the neck and also acts as a veil. This material can also be worn over the turban. Tight fitting caps have draped scarves tied round them, often in a contrasting colour. The women of the Ouled Nail wear turbans hung with gold coins and chains. Bare feet or light sandals of soft leather or babouche slippers are worn.

The men's costume is of a similar style to neighbouring countries', with the long-sleeved cotton djellaba, or the winter version in wool, the thick hooded 'burnous' cloak and loose under-trousers. Men favour white, blue, grey and beige in colours; white is popular as it does not absorb heat and blue is considered to act as an insect repellent.

The central Sahara desert is the home of the nomadic Tuareg tribe, where the men are veiled, but the women are unveiled. When a boy becomes an adult, he receives the blue veil, the 'tagilmus' or 'taguelmoust', which he will wear for the rest of his life. The tagilmus is a strip of indigo blue cotton, 3 m (10 ft) in length, and it is wound round the head in a special way, forming a turban. It covers the eyebrows and the lower part of the face: the lower folds are loose over the mouth and can be lifted for eating. The cotton material used for the loose garments is dyed indigo from plants from the Sudan. It is not a fast dye and easily stains the body, so that the Tuaregs have earned the name 'Blue Men'.

The women wear loose robes dyed blue, but their only head covering is with shawls.

Both men and women wear rather broad, open-toed sandals with thick rawhide soles which give a firm grip on sand and are also a protection against scorpions, sandfleas and thorns.

The Tuareg are great believers in charms, sewing them into clothing, and round the neck is a plaited leather string, attached to which are tiny decorated pouches or little silver boxes. Inside each container there is a sentence or prayer from the Koran.

TUNISIA

Over the centuries the way of life and dress have changed very little for people in Tunisia, especially for those living inland or away from the coastal towns.

Women cover their faces; this is done by draping over their heads and round the body an enveloping loose cotton type of cloak called a 'safsari', or 'sifsari', white in colour for the younger women and black for the older. In the villages the safsari may be of bright colours. This garment not only hides the face but acts as a protection from dust and dirt for the garments worn underneath. In the winter the cotton cloak is replaced by a woollen one, called a haik, which is usually white or grey except in the south, where it is black with red fringes. Away from the towns or public places the safsari is replaced by a simple cotton head covering which is drawn across the face when necessary.

The most popular form of costume is made from a long piece of cotton material, sometimes 5 m (about 6 yds) long, called a 'mellia'. This is draped round the body and fastened on either shoulder with silver pins. A woven belt or sash is tied round the waist. This costume is usually worn over a white or patterned high-necked smock or slip, with either long or short sleeves, called a 'suria' or 'meriol'. Plate 51 illustrates this costume. Dancers will often dispense with the smock so that the draped material forms an arm covering. In many villages women wear a long skirt called a 'futa', which is tied round the waist. The material is often in stripes or checks and this skirt can either be worn with a coloured blouse or over the mellia. Some Bedouin women drape the futa skirt round them to combine an overall costume. Red is the predominant colour, especially among those living in the oases inland and in the olive groves of the east. Blue is popular and is used a great deal in North Africa as it reflects the sky and the sea. A bright yellow is favoured by the women of Zarzis in the south. The Bedouins and the townspeople prefer darker colours such as purple, maroon and blue. In the mountain region of the north-west a vivid purple is worn. Stripes in two colours are popular together with floral patterns and checks.

For special occasions silk is used for the safsari and, as the religious custom demands, the head is covered with a scarf tied round the head. The head-dress shown in Plate 51 is very elaborate and would be worn for a festive occasion.

In the more remote regions and in the south, many of the inhabitants are of Berber extraction and cover the head with a loose, coloured scarf, round which is tied a piece of material similar to a turban in a strong contrasting shade. Straw hats are also worn and on the island of Djerba the straw crowns are made into a peak.

Men wear clothing similar to other North African and Arab countries: there are only slight variations and changes of name. The most popular basic garment is the 'djellaba', or 'jellaba', which is a plain, long-sleeved, ankle length shirt. Over this can be worn a variety of coats. The 'burnous' is a type of cloak or cape made of a thick dark brown wool or camelhair. A hood is attached which is pulled over the head during the winter and also gives protection against sand and wind. Also popular is a long woollen coat, open down the front, which is a substitute for the 'burnous' and is called a 'kachabia' or 'kashabia'. It is often made in black or dark brown woollen material and is striped.

A similar loose fitting coat, which opens only to the waist, is called a 'kadroun'. For the winter months this is made in brown or black wool, but for summer in white or striped cotton; when made in the lighter material it is known as a djebba (see Plate 51). Trousers reaching to the calf are worn underneath the basic garments.

The red fez is worn mostly by the older generation, the younger men preferring the popular 'chechias', which is a tight-fitting round hat made in felt. White turbans are also worn, with an end draped across the neck, or there are straw hats with broad brims known as 'sunshine' or 'mudhala' hats.

In the towns European style shoes or backless slippers are preferred, but in the country areas many go barefooted.

EGYPT

Costumes have changed slightly through the thousands of years of Egypt's history, but the material is still woven on the old style looms: cotton, which is Egypt's major crop, is used extensively for costumes. The women wear a very simple loose dress which can either be gathered into a yoke or be cut straight down without the gathers. The square or round neckline and front opening are decorated with embroidery, braid, beads or pearls, according to the occasion, or can be quite plain. A very elaborate wedding dress from the Siwa oasis in the western desert has buttons sewn on the front in a sun-ray pattern. Coloured thread is also used in the same design—symbolic of the ancient Egyptians' Sun God, Amon Ra.

Numerous necklaces, beads, chains, earrings and bracelets are worn, especially at festivities, together with anklets, a symbol of their bondage to the soil.

Slightly full and loose trousers are worn under the dress and a long veil falls down the back. The veil is attached in front to a dark coloured headband which can be plain or decorated with gold coins. The hair can be plaited and fall each side of the face, but in the desert regions very elaborate hair styles are created and these are covered by a loose black veil. Formerly black was the usual colour for the dress, but now red, blue, green, yellow and white are popular colours.

At one time women would wear an enveloping black taub similar to the cloaks worn in North Africa, which covered the figure from head to toe. If not bare footed, a light sandal is worn.

For men loose fitting, long-sleeved type of shirt known as the 'galabia' was introduced with the coming of the Islamic religion. Made in cotton, this garment can be any colour, striped or plain, but white or blue are the most popular shades. A white cotton shirt can be worn underneath with white loose trousers. Usually the 'galabia' is worn without a belt, but occasionally a red sash is tied round the waist. When working in the fields, the 'galabia' is tied round the waist to give more freedom of movement.

A white turban or a red fez is the most popular form of head covering, or a tight fitting skull cap. Western style shoes are worn in the cities, but in the country it is a type of sandal or feet are bare.

Plate 52 shows a couple dressed in costumes popular in Egypt.

THE LEBANON

Arts and crafts in the Lebanon and the making of material has changed little through the centuries and still continues in the villages. Silk, cotton and wool is woven on hand looms and the dyes are obtained from local materials.

The songs, dances and costumes are divided into three main styles, Dabke, Bedouin and Andalusian. A similar pattern of dress is found within all of the Levant countries and the ethnic links have been maintained in spite of changing boundaries.

The most typical of the Lebanese costume is the Dabke, a style not only worn for dancing, but seen in the villages. The women wear a long-sleeved cotton dress which reaches to just below the knees. Bands of braid decorate the hem and sometimes a short-sleeved jacket is worn. Blue, green, red and pink are the most popular colours, as well as floral patterns. Older people wear a longer skirt. White trousers ending in a frill are always worn. A white or coloured headscarf is tied round the head and knotted at the back. Plate 53 shows a version of this costume used in dancing.

The Bedouins are found both in the Lebanon and Syria and have their own distinctive costume. Women wear a long-sleeved, loose tunic dress reaching to the ankles; it can be plain or have a front panel decorated with gold braid. Red, black, blue and green are all popular colours for these dresses. A long black veil is worn over a red or black pill box hat, or round the head and neck. Another style has a decorated head band which is tied over a long white veil which hangs loosely down the back.

The Andalusian women's costume, so named because of the strong Arab links with Spain, has loose sleeved, knee-length jackets open at the front and sides. Full baggy trousers are worn underneath, with a round-necked, long-sleeved blouse. The red pill box hat has a white veil. Colours vary, the jacket can be pink or dark blue and edged with gold braid with a gold belt. Trousers are usually white or pale blue. With most costumes a low heeled shoe is worn.

The Dabke men wear either very full, black, baggy trousers ending tightly at the knees, or full baggy trousers tucked into calf-length black leather boots. The sides of the trousers are often decorated, but are usually plain for work. High necked, long-sleeved white or coloured shirts are worn, with or without waistcoats, or there are long-sleeved jackets. A deep sash in black, coloured or striped material is tied round the waist.

The Dabke are mountain people and there is a difference of dress between the north and the south. In the south a domed felt hat is worn with a white scarf tied round the edge and knotted at the side (see Plate 53), but in the north, the domed hat is black and worn over a loosely draped black scarf. A white or red fez is also worn and for working a pull-on knitted hat with a crown ending in a little tassel.

The Bedouin costume comprises the loose djellaba in black, blue, grey or striped cotton. A heavy loose 'abaya' is worn over the djellaba and the 'kaffiyeh' headscarf is kept in place by the black agal or head ropes. A flat lightweight sandal is worn.

The Andalusian costume for men consists of full, baggy trousers which are worn with boots, a high-necked, full-sleeved shirt and a short waistcoat.

ETHIOPIA

Ethiopia is a country which is filled with different tribes and racial groups and there is a great variety of costumes.

The most popular form of garment is the 'shamma' which is worn by both men and women. This garment is a long length of material draped round the body; it is made of cotton, calico or muslin, usually white in colour, and can be quite plain or have a deep border woven in geometric designs in bright colours. Women wear the shamma over a long white cotton robe or dress with long sleeves. The hem of the dress sometimes has a woven border which matches that of the shamma. The way the shamma is draped can denote region, status and age. In the north the women drape a lightweight cotton shamma over their heads or let a corner fall down the back in a triangle which often reaches to the hem.

Some of the more elaborate town costumes of former years are not now seen, being replaced by the simple shamma and dresses. Occasionally more affluent women wear a long white robe of thick cotton with a narrow panel of multicoloured embroidery down the front. White is the predominant colour as it does not absorb the heat.

In Harar, a walled city in the highlands, women favour highly coloured shammas. Plate 54 shows a woman from the Aderi tribe from Harar in the province of Haraghe.

The Ataya women wear a loose white cotton dress with a patterned border and dispense with the shamma as it would hide the amber beads, coloured stones and silver balls worn round the neck. They tie coloured scarves round their heads over felt skull caps.

In the more primitive areas of the hot south-west, only a short type skirt is worn with an end draped over the shoulder. Sometimes the naked top of the body is decorated by the wearing of numerous ivory and coloured beads and there are also necklaces made from hair from the tails of giraffes. The lower lips of these women are pierced and from them hang bead necklaces. Bracelets, rings and ear clips are worn by many groups. Silver is the metal usually used although the richer town dwellers might have gold. Christians are identified as such by the wearing of a coloured band round the neck, called a 'mateb'. Ornate crosses made in Coptic or Portuguese designs are also very popular.

The accepted dress for men is a white, long-sleeved tunic shirt worn outside long white trousers, all made in linen or cotton (see Plate 54). They also wear the shamma, sometimes with a woven border. It is draped in different ways according to the region, but the men usually have it over the right shoulder and the women over the left. The draping can also have special significance, such as when attending church, celebrations or visiting someone of high rank. On Feast days, a tunic of striped silk is worn with the shamma.

The various hill and desert tribes wear loose short trousers with shirts or a shamma draped round the body in various ways, either over the shirt or like a toga round the body. In rainy weather, townspeople, both men and women, wear a heavy felt cape which is conical in shape with openings for the arms and hands. Shepherds' capes are made from animal skins and the members of the church are distinguished by a black cape which hangs loosely from the shoulders.

Turbans are worn by many Ethiopians and these are rather high and round in shape; they are made of white cotton, though monks have yellow. Many of the tribes go bareheaded and specialise in elaborate plaited hair, formed into shapes using mud or melted butter.

Both men and women go barefooted or in the towns wear loose sandals of leather or plaited grass.

SAUDI ARABIA

The costumes worn in the cities and towns of Saudi Arabia are similar to those found in other Arab countries. The women wear the long-sleeved, loose fitting, ankle-length dresses in materials ranging from printed cottons or silks to a mixture of both. Over the dress or 'thōb', is worn a large, black, flowing cloak which covers the dress, head and face. Loose fitting trousers are worn under the thōb.

Among the Arabs, both men and women keep both the body and the head well covered. A woman never appears in the streets unveiled and even in her own home the veil is only removed in the presence of her closest relatives and never if men are present. The older women are not required to be so strict, but the custom has become habitual. Younger girls under the age of nine may go unveiled and women may relax the rule of being veiled in the presence of very young boys and very old men. A black face mask often replaces the veil, which allows full use of the hands.

The man's costume is also based on the thōb or tobe. Made in white, blue, grey or beige cotton or linen, it is usually worn with calf-length trousers underneath.

For special occasions a loose-sleeved coat, called a 'gumbāz' or 'kibber', is worn over the thōb and this can be plain, striped or in a rich material, depending upon the affluence of the wearer. A large sleeveless cloak called an 'abāyeh' is also worn. This can be made from cotton, fine wool or a coarse wool woven in stripes or can also be made in a material based on silk with embroidery round the neck and front edges.

A white, knitted skull cap covers the head and over this is worn a head veil or scarf called the 'keffiyeh'. The 'agāl', or head ropes, keep the scarf in place. Headwear can denote social position and the agāl can be very elaborate and made from metal threads.

Footwear for both men and women consists of either sandals or the western-style light shoes, or they go barefooted.

The nomadic tribal groups known as the Bedouin also live in Saudi Arabia. Each tribal group has a slightly different costume which indicates locality, social position and marital status; these are revealed by the embroidery on the women's costume, the head-dress and hair style, the jewellery and the pattern or colour of the material that is used. Red embroidery is only worn by married women and blue by young unmarried girls. The loose thōb, or dress, is often black or blue and highlighted by embroidery round the neck, on the sleeves and along the hem, but these are not for everyday use and the working costume is very plain.

Married women wear a head veil over which is a turban or band which can be decorated with silver coins. Alternatively a head veil or cloak is worn over a turban.

Plate 55 shows a child and her father dressed in the Bedouin costume of Saudi Arabia.

The Bedouin men are less distinctive in their costume and wear the typical Arab thōb, gumbāz and abāyeh. The keffiyeh is often draped under the chin and can be lifted across the face as a protection against sandstorms. In the winter it is crossed under the chin and fixed on top of the head to give warmth.

Women will often be barefooted or wear sandals, but the men, when not barefoot, wear either a western style shoe, ankle boot or sandal.

202

IRAQ

The costumes of Iraq follow a pattern similar to those worn in other Arab countries but with differences in names and styles. In the central and southern regions there is very little change, but the northern tribes of the Kurdish, Turkmen and other smaller groups wear a very distinctive form of dress.

In the ancient capital of Baghdad and the surrounding areas, the women wear a loose tunic dress with long sleeves, not unlike the djellaba, which is called a 'hashimi'. Made in cotton or a blend of cotton and silk, and in various colours, black and green predominate. A floral pattern or geometric design is often woven into the material. As is the custom with Arab women under the Moslem rule, the head and face is covered with a large black cloak or 'abaya'. The cloak is held loosely around the body, enveloping the hashimi, and drawn across the face. Made from a light material, it can also be in fine wool.

The women in the south and central regions wear a hashimi, often decorated around the neck and down the front and sleeve edges. Blue is popular, with white, gold or variously coloured embroidery or braid. Silver or gold bracelets, ear-rings, anklets, nose rings and rows of coloured beads are worn extensively in this region.

The full, black abaya cloak, first worn when a girl comes of age, is an essential part of the costume. Women wear ankle-length full trousers under the hashimi. Shoes are of soft leather and made like a backless slipper or moccasin. The face, neck and body are often tattooed.

Men also have an established style of dress; the loose robes are as have been worn for many centuries. In Baghdad and the surrounding areas a long, white shirt, buttoning from the neck to the waist, and reaching to the ankles, is worn; this is known as a 'dishdasha'. Over this garment is worn a long, cross-over coat called a 'zaboon' or 'saya', which is made in striped or plain coloured materials. Trousers or 'sherwal' are of white cotton and the backless shoes or sandals are of leather.

Over these basic garments a large abaya is worn. Made from camel hair, it is in white, brown or black and can be plain or decorated with braid down the front and on the sleeve opening; this decoration is often very elaborate. A turban or wrapped scarf, known as a 'jarrawiyah', is the traditional head-dress of this region.

In the south and central regions, the dishdasha is worn without the zaboon, especially during hot weather. Colours vary but white, beige or a striped material are worn a great deal. A draped white headscarf, or 'kuffiya', is worn over a white skull cap and is kept in place by a cord, or 'iqal', made of camel hair. This cord can be knotted in various ways and can be in one or two thicknesses. The headscarf can also be in checked cotton of red and white or black and white and is known as a 'yatshmagh'. Different types of scarves denote region, profession and tribe. The footwear and trousers worn are similar to those found in Baghdad.

The Kurdish people in the north have many different styles, according to the tribe. The women's costume is based on the long, loose hashimi, made in coloured cottons in stripes and worn with or without a belt or sash. A scarf is draped round the head and face over which is placed a coloured turban. The turban can be fringed or hung with jewellery and coins. There are many different styles of head-dresses.

Men wear a loose, long-sleeved jacket over a shirt. A broad sash is tied over full and baggy trousers. These trousers and jackets can be white, black, blue or striped. The turban is tied with a fringed edge. Lightweight leather moccasins or sandals are worn. Plate 55 illustrates a Kurdish man in summer clothes made of coarse cotton. His felt hat has a scarf wrapped round it with a feather tucked into it, a sign that it is a festive occasion.

ISRAEL

Israel is a country which is now both old and new. Jews came from many countries to settle in Israel and each group brought with them different ethnic cultures which blended with the ancient traditions. Also living in the country are Arabs and Druzes.

Jewish communities throughout the world have always worn a very distinctive form of dress and over three hundred different costumes are housed in the Haaretz Museum in Tel Aviv. However, they are an inheritance from particular groups and countries and are not really representative of the new nation. A costume was therefore evolved to suit the folk culture which developed and folk groups which represent Israel wear either the old or the new.

The old style is shown in the Yemenite costume based on those worn by the Jews who returned to Israel from the Yemen. This costume is typical of a desert community and has only changed slightly through the years.

The women wear a calf length, loose, black tunic which has long sleeves and a high neckline. A decorated and embroidered panel extends down the front. Black cotton trousers are worn under the tunic and the head-dress consists of a tightly-fitting black hood, richly decorated with braid and gold coins. Alternatively a loose white or coloured headscarf is worn over a band or other coloured scarf tied round the head.

The men wear a loose, white cotton, calf-length tunic with a broad belt round the waist and a white turban on the head. Both men and women go either barefooted or wear light sandals. There are many variations of these costumes.

The modern costume is simple in design; the girls wear a short, knee-length, full skirted dress with wide loose sleeves. Coloured braid decorates the dress in a variety of ways, according to the group. The braid can be round the hem of the skirt and the sleeves, on the neckline or down the front.

The men wear a loose shirt, worn outside the trousers and this costume is also braided in various ways. No head-dress is worn and dancers usually perform barefooted. Plate 56 illustrates a couple wearing modern costumes.

The Arabs wear their traditional garments. A shepherd has a white cotton shirt, or galabia, fastened round the waist with a leather belt. A black 'abaya' coat of camel hair or wool is worn for warmth and on his head a white scarf is held in place with black cord. The scarf can be loose or tied in turban fashion. Women wear a loose black tunic style of dress, often with a band of material tied as a belt. A square panel of embroidery is at the neck and a white scarf covers the head. Black trousers are worn under the tunic and, when not barefooted, a light sandal is worn.

SRI LANKA

The costume worn throughout the island of Sri Lanka is very simple in design.

Women wear either a cotton wrap-over sarong or a sari. The sarong reaches from the waist to the ankle and is worn with a tight-fitting, short-sleeved blouse. The sari is a long length of material gathered into the waist with one end draped over the left shoulder of the blouse. Colours vary considerably, the sarong and blouse can be white or the two garments can be in contrasting colours, pinks, blues and pastel shades being very popular. No hats or head-dresses are worn but, when necessary, the sari is draped over the head. The tea plantation workers often cover their heads with a wide white headscarf as protection against the sun and this helps to support the straps of the collecting baskets on the backs, the straps passing across the head.

Men also wear the cotton sarong, with or without a loose white shirt, according to the occupation of the wearer. White is worn a great deal and the men also favour checks for the sarong, although colours are seldom strong or violent. No head covering is worn and both men and women go either barefoot or wear a light sandal.

Plate 57 illustrates costumes worn by Kandyan dancers. These dances are mainly for men, and the woman wears the counterpart to the man's costume. Fine cotton material is gathered into a waistband and held in place by the heavy ornamental belt. The woman wears a loose draped 'dhoti' below two layers of braided outerskirts. The man wears white cotton trousers under his gathered skirt; they are tight fitting round the ankles and lower calves. The breastplate is of braid, silver discs and beads and the pattern varies with each dancer. The head-dress is also of silver.

INDIA

India's artistic traditions, which are deeply rooted in religion, greatly influenced music, customs, dance, festivals and associated costume.

The most popular form of dress for women is the sari, worn in numerous ways depending upon the province. At one time the sari also denoted caste. This garment consists of a length of material, 5–9 metres in length and 105 cm in width. Made in a variety of materials such as cotton, muslin, silk or nylon, it can be simple in pattern or very elaborate, depending upon the occasion. The sari is worn over a tight-fitting, half-sleeved or sleeveless bodice called a 'choli' (see Plate 58). A long petticoat is worn which reaches to the ankles and is tied at the waist with a draw-string. The sari is wrapped round the petticoat, pleated in front and tucked into the top. The long end, the 'pallu', is draped over the left shoulder. The pallu can also be draped over the head or tucked into the waist on the left side to form a drape.

Indian cotton has been made for thousands of years and is the most popular of materials used today. Patterns, colours and fabrics vary according to the regions: colours are obtained from vegetable and mineral dyes and are strong in tone. The border of the sari and the final metre is decorated in patterns, mostly based on living forms. The elephant, peacock, lotus, mango, buffalo and various trees are some of the shapes that are incorporated into patterns. Some of the most elaborate patterns are made in gold, so that when the sari is finished it is burnt and the metal recovered.

Varanasi is well known for its fine silk saris with the borders often brocaded in silver and gold. Kashmir weaves saris in the famous designs which influenced the Scottish paisley shawls of the nineteenth century. Pochampalli silk saris have the whole material covered with ancient patterns. From Sanganer, handblocked printed muslin saris are made: from Chanderi there are the cotton saris. A very light silk sari is made in Tassar which is woven from the cocoon of the wild silk moth.

In the south the sari can be worn in a coorgi style with the pleats at the back. When working on the land, the sari is pulled through the legs to form a type of trouser and the pallu is draped over the right shoulder.

Brides wear a very elaborate sari, usually in red and with a green choli. Draped over their head is a long piece of red material, or 'chuni', which is decorated.

In some of the northern regions, very full skirts called 'ghagra' are worn with a choli and a long length of material like a stole, known as a dupatta, is wrapped round the head and shoulders. In Kashmir and the Punjab, coloured loose tunics are worn over trousers. This type of costume can replace the sari and is worn mainly by the Moslems both in India and Pakistan. The knee-length tunic called a 'kamecz' or a slightly looser style known as a 'kurta', are both worn over 'salwar' (trousers). The trousers are often gathered in at the ankles and are popular with young girls.

The men's costume is based on the 'dhoti', a length of material in cotton or silk printed with or without a border. This is tied or wrapped round the lower part of the body in numerous ways, according to the region. When working on the land it can be pulled through the legs and tied to form a loose trouser. A shirt or loose tunic covers the upper body or just a long dupatta is worn, wrapped round the shoulders and chest. Tight white trousers, or 'churidar', with smart button-through, knee-length jackets, or shirwani, are worn by the Sikhs (see Plate 58), whilst the Punjabi men wear white shirts over a coloured dhoti, a black sleeveless waistcoat and an elaborate turban. Round the neck is a string of yellow beads. Turbans are worn in many regions and the Sikhs wear them to cover their hair which, for religious reasons, is never cut.

Muslim men wear a dark round hat and on special occasions, little boys wear velvet ones decorated with braid and beads.

Throughout India both men and women are generally either barefooted or wear open sandals.

In complete contrast are the costumes worn by the classical dancers. Religious in inspiration, the best known style of dancing is that of the classical Bharat Natyam, which comes from the south. The dancer wears a pleated sari which is draped and fastened in such a way as to allow for movement. Plate 59 illustrates two of these dancers. Kathakali, an ancient dance from Kerala, has the most elaborate of all costumes. Essentially a dance for men, about twenty-four ankle-length skirts are worn with a decorated red wool or cotton jacket, a long white scarf with white and red cotton lotus blooms on the end and a large head-dress shaped like a temple with a halo, studded with gold and jewels.

The Kathak style of the north consists of both men and women wearing full, gathered or pleated ghagra skirts with a choli for the women and a long-sleeved jacket for the man. Both sexes wear tight-fitting trousers, ankle bells and, often, the traditional forage or topi cap.

One of the most beautiful costumes comes from the east and is worn by the Manipuri dancers. Dark orange or green skirts are stiffened from thigh to ankle and decorated with gold thread embroidery; tiny mirrors are also added. Over the skirt is worn a short, silver gauze, gathered skirt edged with a golden border. A coloured choli is worn with a fine gauze veil draped over a special hair style. Belts and jewellery complete this costume.

TIBET

The country of Tibet is divided into three main regions, Kham in the east, Amdo in the north-east and Utsang in the centre.

In each region the costumes differ although the basic garment and style remain the same. There are two kinds of costume, those worn for special ceremonies and festivals and those for everyday use. Silk and fine cotton are used for special clothes, silk being imported from China and cotton from India. Wool is the only material that Tibetans produce and this is used for everyday clothing and for winter wear. Cotton is used in the summer months.

A material called shema is also made from the wool and this fine material is particularly durable and worn by the wealthier families. The finest wool is washed by hand and the coarser by the feet. The clothes of the Lamas have always been woven by men. Various dyes are used for both the wool and the imported cotton: indigo from India and red from madder or obtained from an insect dye in Bhutan. Yellow is obtained from rhubarb and when blended with indigo produces various shades of green. Walnuts provide brown stain and 'off black' is often used.

The basic garment is a long-sleeved coat called a chubba or 'chupa', which is folded across the body and held in place by an attached belt. Both men and women wear this garment and both have the draping from left to right, as is customary in Asia.

The women wear the chupa to the ankles and the drape, hem and edge of the sleeve can have a band of contrasting colour. Underneath the chupa, the women wear two blouses, one with very long sleeves and the other with slightly shorter sleeves. The long sleeves are folded back for work, but for dancing and other occasions hang loosely. The blouses have high necks and one is often rolled over the other to form a collar. Women from the Utsang region wear a chupa without sleeves which allows the long sleeves of the blouse to be shown; this costume is shown in Plate 60. In the summer, Kampas women from the Kham wear only the left sleeve of the chupa, the empty right sleeve being tucked into the waist. This fashion shows the contrasting sleeve of the blouse. Amdo women also follow this style. Decorated boots in felt and leather show just below the skirt and in Kham the boots have very turned-up toes. In winter, warm sheepskin hats decorated with fur are worn but in the summer they will often go bareheaded.

The men's chupa always has sleeves and can be made from wool, cotton or patterned silk, according to the season of the year or the occasion. This chupa also has very long sleeves which are folded back as required. The chupa is ankle length, but can be pulled up over a belt, giving a loose blouse effect. Young men tend to wear their chupas shorter, as do the men from Kham, who wear them knee-length, and those from Amdo, who have them just below the knee. The chupa is worn during the summer months in the same style as that of the women, with the empty right sleeve tucked into the belt and showing a high-necked linen or cotton shirt with long sleeves. Loose baggy trousers are tucked into decorated felt or leather boots. Large sheepskin hats are very popular as are those made from fox, wolf or mink fur.

AFGHANISTAN

Cotton and wool are the main materials used in Afghanistan and these are woven and dyed and made into garments by each family or group. In common with other Muslim countries, the women are veiled, especially in the cities and towns although more recently this custom has been relaxed. However, the very full 'chadri', which covers a woman from head to foot, with a latticed slit for the eyes, is still to be seen. The chadri is made of cotton in shades of blue, brown or black. In the country the women working on the land dispense with this, but cover their faces or hide themselves in the presence of strangers.

The women near the Pakistan border wear long, full trousers, often red in colour, with a loose, long-sleeved tunic dress, rather like the kameez, together with a draped headscarf. This is the basis of many of the women's costumes and the tunic varies in length and design.

In the northern areas striped material is used, often dyed red from madder or in shades of blue and brown. Loose, sleeveless, hip-length jackets are worn or a full-length striped coat for warmth.

Young girls go bareheaded, but women cover their heads with long headscarves, the colours varying according to the groups to which they belong. The scarves are tied round the head, leaving a long end hanging down the back, which can be drawn across the face. A white headscarf signifies the married status.

Children are often barefooted, but adults wear sandals or a form of boot as protection against the rough mountainous ground or earth. The hide comes from the shaggy Yak, which is found throughout the highlands of central Asia.

At puberty the girls of the nomadic Kushi group are given a dress which they must never take off, not even to wash it. As they grow, bands of material are added to the hem. If marriage or some other circumstances provides a new dress, it is worn over the old one, giving a bulky appearance.

The men wear a thigh-length, long-sleeved shirt which is belted at the waist with a skirt effect to the lower half. A sleeveless waistcoat is worn over the shirt and there are loose fitting white trousers. The man in Plate 60 is dressed in this costume.

Another form of dress is the long-sleeved, ankle length 'chupan'. This is a long coat made in wool, often white in colour and worn by the mountain people in the winter months. The chupan is worn over loosely fitting jackets and trousers, or is wrapped round the body like a cloak. There is also a similar type of coat which is made in stripes of darkish colours. In the winter thick woollen, hand-knitted stockings are worn with leather boots. In the cities, the open toe sandal is very common and sometimes shoes with up-pointed toes are seen. There are various forms of headgear which include the large turbans with a long end hanging down the back, neat round astrakan hats, woollen knitted hats and large fur sheepskin hats.

CHINA

The far-flung communities of the People's Republic of China each maintain their own cultural traditions, and songs, dances and costumes are preserved by the Central Institute for Nationalities.

In the east and in the large cities and towns both men and women wear the blue or grey, long-sleeved, cotton denim jacket and trousers which are padded with cotton in winter, giving the jackets a quilted look. Children wear coloured jackets, often in bright red. Peaked caps are very popular. Simple lightweight shoes are worn.

In the five southern provinces the Maio, Tung and Yao people wear different costumes although all are based on trousers and jackets. Women favour black trousers; Tung women have a band of white together with green and white braid round the edge of the trousers, A hip length, pale green jacket is worn tied round the waist with a black sash which has embroidered ends and a long white fringe. Jacket sleeves are also decorated with white braid. A white turban is tied round the head. White socks and red sandals are popular.

Maio women wear calf-length trousers over which is a short black skirt, a maroon or coloured jacket and a striped apron. These women are also distinguished by the wearing of tight gaiters reaching from the knees to the ankles.

Yao women wear hip-length, black jackets or tunics split at the sides; a coloured sash is tied round the waist. Red, white and blue braid decorates the hem and the split seams. They wear pointed black hats and down the front of the jackets silver plaques are fastened. When working in the rice fields, they are barefooted and the trousers are gathered into a band at the ankles. Cotton is mainly used and the embroidery and braiding is made in a cross-stitch pattern. There are numerous costume variations.

Men follow a similar pattern of dress with a tunic jacket and loose trousers. Jackets vary in length and are tied round the waist with a coloured sash making the costume both serviceable and economical. Large straw hats are worn both by men and women and the men wear either light shoes or go barefooted.

The costumes of the north show a complete contrast to those of the south. In the Inner Mongolian Autonomous Region, their costumes reflect their way of life as well as the terrain. The clothes are simple, adaptable and designed for riding. Both men and women wear a similar style of dress and there is an extensive use of wool for clothing.

Dark blues or reds are the popular colours for the coats (or dels) and a bright green or coloured sash is tied round the waist. The hem and the neck of the coat is sometimes braided in a contrasting colour. In the summer or for dancing and special occasions, the del is made of brightly coloured cotton or silk, with contrasting decorations and trousers. Round felt hats are decorated with coloured beads. The men wear sheepskin or astrakan hats or round woollen ones. There are also felt hats with brims. Plate 61 illustrates a woman in the costume of this region.

In the Sinkiang Vighur Autonomous region in the far west, many different nationalities are found: the largest groups are the Moslem Vighurs and Kazakhs. The former group are mainly agricultural while the latter are pastoral and more equestrian. Vighur women wear the loose style, long-sleeved tunic dress in shades of dark red or in patterns of purple and white. Over the dress is a black or dark coloured sleeveless waistcoat. Brightly coloured embroidered skull caps are worn. The long hair is plaited, the married women have two plaits and the younger girls have a number of plaits, according to age.

Men wear long tunic coats in stripes or plain colours and the older men favour darker shades. A triangular folded scarf is tied round the waist. Long trousers are worn with slippers, or are tucked into boots.

Plate 61 shows a Yis man from the Szechwan–Yunnan border in the south west of China. A modern touch is introduced by the lace-up canvas shoes.

Kazakh women are distinguished by their long colourful dresses which have three or four rows of frills at the hem. Over the dress is a knee-length, fitted, long-sleeved coat. Married women wear black or dark colours and the young ones are in stripes of green, orange and white. Their shoes have slightly turned-up toes. Married women wear a long white headscarf folded across the front of the head and with the ends hanging down the back. Younger women wear embroidered, round, velvet hats with a feather in the back and the hair is in a long plait. Light, low-heeled shoes are very popular.

The men are also very colourful in long, loose trousers, short, hip-length, decorated jackets and dark coloured turbans. They wear lightweight shoes.

In complete contrast are the people of the two large islands, Taiwan and Hainan where the people go barefooted and a short, tight, sarong-type skirt is worn. The women are fine weavers and weave cotton, hemp and palm fibres on primitive looms. In Hainan intricate coloured designs are woven into the dark skirts and on the jackets of the men.

The women of Taiwan prefer brightly coloured skirts with less pattern; these are often worn over calf-length trousers.

THAILAND

Silk has been spun and woven in Thailand for nearly two thousand years and the country is famous for its Thai silk in peacock colours of turquoise, gold, scarlet and flame.

Working clothes are made in cotton and silk is used for special or festive occasions. Thai women wear the wrap-round type of sarong skirt, or 'prasin', together with a neat fitting, long-sleeved jacket. In the north a draped sash or 'sabai' is worn over the left shoulder.

On the klongs of Bangkok is the floating market in which the women sell their fruit and vegetables from low-sided boats. They wear brightly coloured prasin and loose-fitting, hip-length jackets, blue being a particularly favourite colour. They wear specially shaped straw hats to protect themselves from the sun.

On the land and in the rice fields, a black jacket and prasin is the usual garb and the women tuck the material through their legs to form a kind of trouser.

The region around Chiangmi in the north is very different from Bangkok. It is the centre of folk art and they make silver jewellery, painted paper umbrellas and a fabric which is a mixture of Thai silk and cotton. The prasin here are distinguished by woven borders and coloured stripes, which are in contrast to the plain material worn in the south.

Costumes worn by the hill tribes consist of black jackets with plain or brightly striped sleeves, black skirts, black trousers, long coloured panels, rather like aprons, wide sashes and short skirts, worn with gaiters reaching from ankle to knee. There is also a bright red costume.

Each tribe has a distinctive head-dress: close fitting hats which are decorated with silver coins, beads, woollen pom poms and fringes. Sometimes the hats are kept in place by means of chains under the chin. Round the neck hang large silver rings, necklaces and chains with silver discs attached. Silver linked belts are worn over sashes and jackets.

The men follow a similar pattern of dress to the women, with a loose shirt or jacket worn over the sarong type of skirt. When working in the fields, black calf-length trousers are worn with a black shirt and a black and white scarf tied round the head, or a straw hat.

For folk dancing the tunic shirt and trousers are in shades of blue, red or gold, with a sash tied round the waist.

In the hills of the north, black predominates and there is a variety of costumes based on long black trousers, black jackets and coloured sashes.

One of the most beautiful of Thailand's costumes are those worn by classical dancers (Plate 62). The girl wears a tight-fitting under-jacket and her skirt, or 'panung', which is made of silk, silver or gold brocade, is 2.7 metres long and 1 metre wide. The panung is pleated in front and held in place by a belt. A broad velvet cape, pailletted and jewelled, fastens to the belt in front and hangs down behind nearly to the hem of the panung. A broad, jewelled, collar, armlets, necklace and bracelets complete the costume with the temple-style head-dress, or 'tchedah'. Before a performance the dancers are sewn into their costumes. A costume is very heavy due to the jewels and metal thread and can weigh as much as 18 kg.

The boy wears an even more elaborate costume with a tight-fitting silver thread brocade jacket with epaulettes and a richly embroidered collar. From a belt hang embroidered panels, and his calf-length trousers are made of silk. His gilt and jewelled head-dress is slightly different in shape from that of his partner and he wears a tassel on the right side whilst the girl has one on the left.

Dancers are bare footed, but most Thais wear a western style shoe or a type of sandal. Shoes are always removed when entering a house.

KOREA

As with their near neighbours in the west, Koreans have bred silkworms for centuries. As each family has to be self-supporting, the cotton, silk and hemp required for costumes is woven in the homes. Cotton is used for most clothes with hemp for hard-wearing garments and for the very poor; silk is only used for occasions such as weddings or special celebrations and then stored away.

Young girls, children and the Kisang (the professional entertainers), wear brightly coloured costumes, often in reds and yellows. The young women favour pastel shades of pink, blue and aquamarine and the older women wear mostly white, although it is a colour which can signify mourning. The period of mourning is for three years and so it becomes a predominant colour and is often worn continuously.

The use of colour is important in Korea and is associated with five points or directions. North is represented by the colour black; south is red; west is white; east is blue; and the centre is yellow.

Women's costume consists of a high-waisted skirt gathered into a yolk, the dress being called a 'chima'. A petticoat, or 'sokchima', cut in the same style is worn underneath, together with loosely cut trousers. A high-waisted overblouse or jacket, the 'chogori', is tied on the right side with a bright ribbon. Plate 62 illustrates a small girl dressed in this costume. In Korea both the men and the women fasten their garments from the left to right. White socks and small black slippers are worn.

For a wedding the chima, made of silk, is very colourful, for example, in red with an overblouse of green with bands of red and yellow on the sleeves. A beaded crown is worn from which hang long coloured ribbons which fall down the back and are decorated with jewels.

Mothers carry their babies on their backs by wrapping round themselves a bright red, pink, green or black quilt into which the baby is placed.

Men wear white baggy trousers called 'paji', which end in cuffs fastened at the ankles. A white shirt with loose sleeves is worn under a sleeveless white or black waistcoat which buttons up the front. A pocket hangs from the trousers' waistband. For very formal occasions a long white coat, the 'torumagi', is worn.

Straw hats are usual and there is an old style black horsehair hat shaped like a Welsh woman's head-dress.

Farmers celebrate festive occasions with folk dances and songs and decorate their costumes with bands of coloured material. Over their white waistcoats, in a cross pattern, they tie bright green, yellow, red or pink bands with a coloured sash round the waist. A band of red material is tied round the forehead and knotted in a bow over the left eye. They also wear an unusual hat with a round, turned-up brim which is held on the head with a band under the chin. On the crown of the hat is a tuft of crane's feathers fixed to a swivel button; the wearer can swing the feathers with a movement of the head. The feathers are sometimes replaced with long paper streamers.

JAPAN

There are four types of dress to be found in Japan: those for everyday use, those for special or festive occasions, the work clothes for those on the land and the very elaborate costumes worn for the Noh and Kabuki plays.

The materials used are linen, cotton and silk. Linen is the oldest material known to Japan; at one time flax was grown and woven by almost every family. There have been great changes since the production of modern materials, patterns and colours. Young people tend to wear bright colours and the older generation favour darker tones. Traditional patterns represent the characteristic features of the country and the seasons.

For everyday wear both men and women wear the kimono. This garment dates back to the twelfth century and remains a practical and elegant dress for modern times. Although not suitable for city wear, for which western styles are favoured, within the home a simple kimono is usually worn. The very informal kimono has shorter sleeves than the more conventional garment. In the summer the kimono is made of a light cotton and is known as a yukata and is worn over an undergarment. In the spring and autumn the kimono is lined and in the winter it is padded and worn over a cotton yukata. A short coat known as a haori, which is sometimes lined, is also worn over the kimono in winter, for formal occasions or when out of doors.

The long-sleeved kimono, or furisode, was originally for children, but is now also worn by unmarried ladies. Married women's sleeves are shortened and children's kimonos are made with tucks along the shoulders and around the waist which are let out as the child grows. The kimono is always folded in a special way before being placed in a drawer. Silk kimonos are always very carefully cleaned; the garment is unpicked and each piece cleaned separately before being resewn. Cotton is the most popular material for everyday use but is replaced for special occasions by silk. No buttons are used in the fastening of the kimono and they are draped across the body from left to right and held in place by a deep sash known as an obi. The obi was at one time very elaborate and was tied in a variety of ways. The present day obi measures 6 m (2 ft) by about 4 m (13 ft), is doubled over lengthwise and sewn along one edge. A more informal obi of 15 cm (6 in) in width is tied more easily in a less complicated design. A narrow unlined obi is worn with the summer lightweight yukata and a narrow lined one for everyday cotton kimonos.

The obi is always tied at the back, but in some regions is tied at the front for funerals and worn with a black kimono decorated with family crests.

At her wedding a bride wears a very elaborate kimono; over a white or pastel coloured kimono, either patterned or embroidered, is worn a long-sleeved furisode in the same material. Sometimes there is a second coat over the furisode. The bride's hair is specially dressed and a white or pastel hat, decorated at the back with flowers and with flat sides, is fixed on to the complicated hair style. These elaborate hair styles are now only seen on special occasions or are worn by the geishas.

White socks with a split toe, called tabi, are worn with all kimonos, both by men and women.

The most popular form of footwear is the wooden geta or the zori The geta was originally designed to keep the feet clean in the muddy streets. The flat wooden sole is supported by two lateral slats and the shoe is kept on by two thongs which pass between the first and second toes and divide over the top of the foot.

The zori have flat soles of woven straw, rush, flax and bamboo, covered with a material or leather. A similar thonging to the geta keeps the shoe on the foot. They are now worn by both men and women as formal footwear to match ceremonial kimonos.

Plate 63 shows a Japanese couple dressed for an important occasion. The woman wears a kimono in silk and tied round her waist is the long obi.

The man wears the ceremonial kimono made in dark blue silk. Over the basic kimono he wears a pleated divided skirt made in very fine stripes. Known as the hakama it was once always worn by courtiers and the samurai. A loose coat with his family crest embroidered in white is worn over the kimono and hakama. A belt is worn round the hips and round his neck is a silken cord with the two tasselled ends tied in a special way.

The informal kimono for a man is made of cotton and is usually black, brown, grey or dark blue. Fine checks, polka dots or bird's eye design are also used. A belt is worn low on the hips and the sleeves are shorter than those for the women.

The basic work garment for women consists of a long-sleeved blouse or coat, loose trousers or mompe, a wide straw hat worn over a coloured or white headscarf and either bare feet, plaited straw sandals or waraji, the wooden geta or the jak tabi, a sock which has a durable rubber sole. There are many variations, according to region.

The coat can reach to the hips or be longer and split at the sides. Sometimes a kimono is worn and the skirt tucked into the obi, showing the working trousers or a white underskirt over the trousers, rather like an apron. Cuffs are often worn as a protection to the sleeves. Blue and white checked squares or patterned cotton material is very popular with white, blue or striped trousers.

The head is covered by either the wide hat made from sedge, bark, bamboo and reeds, or a white or coloured headscarf.

For work men wear the short, dark blue cotton hopi coat or a loose shirt over trousers and they also wear the same wide brimmed hat and footwear as the women. In the wet season special rainproof capes, made from straw, are worn.

Some of the most elaborate costumes are to be seen in the Kabuki and Noh theatres. All the roles are played by men and the costumes, which have not changed for hundreds of years, are handed down through each actor's family.

The Gagaku-Bugaka court entertainment, which came to Japan from China in the seventh century, has very elaborate costumes; the musicians wear the white robes and black helmets of the Chinese Tang dynasty and the dancers wear brocade robes and wide, richly patterned trousers which are similar to skirts.

Romanian double apron

Gaiter worn by women in S.W. China, Burma and Thailand

Man's sleeve from Mezökövesd, Hungary

Silver fibula pins, jewellery and head-dress from North Africa

Man's waistcoat from Ibiza

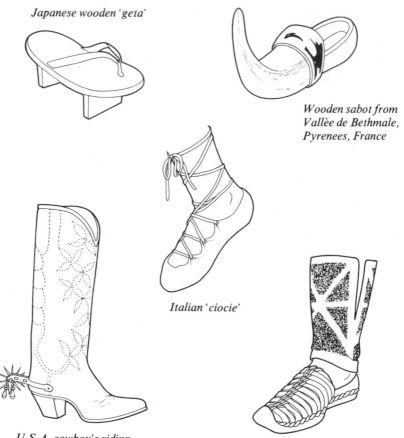

Japanese wooden 'geta'

Wooden sabot from Vallèe de Bethmale, Pyrenees, France

Italian 'ciocie'

U.S.A. cowboy's riding boot

Yugoslavian 'opinci'

South American sandal

THE PHILIPPINES

The music, dances and costumes found throughout the islands of the Philippines reflect their many ethnic influences.

The most popular costumes worn by the women are the Balintawak style and the Patadiong. The Balintawak consists of an ankle-length, full-skirted dress in white or a pale coloured cotton. The bodice has a round 'boat neck' and short, wide, puffed sleeves. Over the dress is worn a second, but shorter, skirt in a contrasting colour which can be in large checks, a floral pattern or in stripes. The over-skirt is draped round the waist, in a V line with the point reaching nearly to the hem of the dress. The loose end falls over the left shoulder. The Patadiong consists of a sarong-type skirt worn with a blouse and is illustrated in Plate 64.

No shoes are worn with either costume except in the rainy season when wooden shoes, called bakya, are used. The women go bareheaded, except when working on the land or in the rice fields where a large brimmed hat of woven bamboo and palm leaves, called a salakot, is worn.

In the mountain regions of the large northern island of Luzon, the Ilocano and Ifugao women wear short, tight-fitting, hand-woven skirts in colourful horizontal stripes, and outside these are white short-sleeved blouses and striped loose jackets. A coloured band is tied round the head and they go barefooted.

One of the most attractive costumes is known as the 'Maria Clara' style; based on the old style of dress it shows European influence. Made in silk, fine cotton or taffeta, the full floor length skirt will often have a train. White or pastel shades of blues, pinks and mauve are used or a broad stripe in a dark contrasting colour, black on white or deep maroon on pale pink. The skirt is worn with a blouse of the same pale shade, the wide loose sleeves reach to the wrists, and around the shoulders and the 'boat neck' a silk fichu or shawl is draped and caught at the waist. There are several versions of this style, some with very elaborate flower embroidery decorated with beads and pearls. The dress is often referred to as a serpentina, siete cuchillos or paloma. With this costume low heeled shoes are worn.

In the Muslim south the costume reflects the Malayan background of the people. A gathered wrap-over or sarong type of ankle-length skirt is worn with a long-sleeved jacket fastening up the front to a V neck.

Jacket and skirt are in contrasting colours of blues, pinks and greens, and the women go barefooted.

The men's costumes are known as Barong Tagalog and consist of long cotton trousers and white, long-sleeved shirts worn outside the trousers (see Plate 66).

When the women wear the Balintawak style, the trousers are red or black with a white shirt. With the Patadiong style, trousers and shirt are both white. To accompany the Maria Clara costume, the trousers are black and the white shirt or camisa de chino is extra long. Black shoes are worn with this formal costume, but the men are usually barefooted.

Wooden bakya, in various shapes and sizes are worn in wet weather, but only in the villages and poorer areas. The men will sometimes wear a straw buli or balangot hat similar to a flat-topped Spanish Cordobés hat.

The mountain tribesmen wear only a loin cloth woven in horizontal stripes. The Ilongots have a plain dark blue or black cloth, with a coloured band wound round the hips. A long red or black band is tied round the head and no shoes are worn.

The men in the south wear an ankle-length sarong or skirt, in checked cotton with a loose coloured shirt or jacket. A scarf is tied round the head and knotted at the side and they go barefooted.

INDONESIA

There are seven major areas in the archipelago of Indonesia: Sumatra, which is the largest of the islands; Java, which accounts for more than half of the population; the Nusa Tenggara group (which includes Bali), Kalimantan, Sulawesi (the third largest island), Maluku and Irian Barat.

The most popular form of costume for both men and women is the long wrap-around skirt called a kain which varies in colour, design and material according to the region. It can be worn gathered or pleated in front, or wrapped across. Cotton is generally used as this is grown and woven on the islands.

Indonesia is renowned for its famous Batik designs, especially in Java where the material is patterned and dyed by an intricate process involving the use of layers of wax. Some designs and colours were at one time reserved only for court circles.

For special occasions the kain is woven with metal thread, an expensive process as the metal has to be imported. The very elaborate kains used for weddings are passed down as heirlooms.

Over the kain the women wear a long-sleeved jacket called a kebaya. In Sumatra this resembles a long loose tunic which reaches to the knees and is worn with a length of material folded and draped over the right shoulder, known as the sabai.

On Timor, the kebaya is hip length, sleeveless and worn with a belt. The sabai is draped round the shoulders and tucked under the belt.

In Bali a broad coloured sash is worn round the waist over a short kebaya. When working in the rice fields the women wear very large, umbrella shaped bamboo hats, known as chapil. In towns the women are usually bare-headed or have a simple head covering of draped cotton or muslin. The Minangkabau women of western Sumatra wear head-dresses of folded material which form two points.

Plate 65 shows a girl from the island of Bali wearing the costume of the Legong dancers. A long kain about 1.8 metres long is wrapped round the body and reaches from the chest to the ankles. A deep torso band is wrapped round the body. The long apron, collar and hip ornament which hangs at the back are all made of soft leather painted gold. The head-dress is also made from leather which has been cut into patterns and painted. White frangipani flowers decorate the leather crown and these are attached to tiny springs which tremble as the dancer moves. Emerald green, magenta, purple, gold, cerise, yellow and deep blue are the colours used in the costumes.

The men's costume is fairly simple and consists of a kain worn with a white shirt or a loose jacket in a variety of colours which is worn over the skirt. Baggy trousers are also worn, especially in Sumatra.

Headgear varies and can denote rank as well as region. A chieftain of a village will tie a cotton turban in a special way: on Bali the turban is knotted in front; in Java certain officials knot it at the back. Straw hats of different shapes and sizes vary within the islands, the popular round black hat or pitji is universal. Mostly the men are barefooted apart from those who wear western style dress.

BURMA

The most popular costume for both men and women in Burma is the long wrap-round skirt or longyi. This is worn folded across the front and can be gathered in, the men tying it in a knot and the women tucking in the ends. A shirt or blouse is worn with the longyi or a type of shirt-jacket called an eingyi which is worn outside. Cotton is chiefly used although silk is also worn, or a mixture of both cotton and silk.

Plate 65 shows a Burmese dancer wearing one of the costumes based on the old court style. The tight-fitting skirt, or longyi, reaches from the waist to the calf. On to the hem of the skirt is added a deep section of fine white cotton or organdie which flows into a train. The upper bodice is sleeveless although sometimes sleeves are worn. A white cotton, transparent jacket is worn over the bodice. Pastel colours are usual for this type of costume and pale blues and pinks are very popular. White socks are worn and sometimes sandals.

When working outdoors both men and women wear large, flat, straw hats. The men also tie a coloured handkerchief, often in the same material as the longyi, round their heads.

In the Shan territory men are distinguished by broad cotton turbans in white or in coloured stripes and squares. The women have a folded white headscarf or turban. The most popular form of footwear is the flat, open sandal held on the feet by two straps.

In the Kachin region, very attractive costumes are worn by the women consisting of black skirts edged with a red panel tied round the waist with a blue sash. Black, long-sleeved jackets are worn over white or black blouses and numerous strings of small red, blue and yellow beads cover the chest.

Tall, black hats are worn and large circular silver ear-rings. A type of gaiter reaching from knee to ankle is a feature of many of the Kachin costumes. In the same region, bright red skirts woven with a yellow border and pattern are fastened round the hips with belts of cane. Over a black jacket is a huge collar, made of silver discs, which covers the shoulders, chest and the upper part of the back. Silver ornaments, like a fringe, hang from the edge of the collar. Red gaiters match the skirt and the usual open sandals are worn.

The Lashi women, also from Kachin, wear similar costumes, but in blue and white with blue turbans and red bead necklaces. The women from the tribe known as Black Lisu wear a tight-fitting cap made from strings of red beads and white buttons and with tiny brass bells across the forehead.

Very unusual costumes are worn by the Padaung women who live in the hills of the Kayah region; these are one of the eight main ethnic tribes and Padaung means 'long neck'. The women are often described as giraffe necked as they have numerous brass rings round their necks. A long neck is much admired and at a special ceremony and feast, called a Waso, held when the moon is full, little girls of five have their first brass ring put round their necks. As times goes on, more and more are added until the total can reach twenty-one. Brass rings are also placed round their legs, extending from the ankles to above the knees.

The costume worn is very simple, with a short, dark blue skirt edged with red, a loose white tunic trimmed with red and a short blue jacket. For working there is a plain cotton, short-sleeved smock. A headscarf is draped round the head, forming a type of turban.

Other tribes in the same region wear more colourful costumes, but above the calf and around each knee steel wire is coiled or, alternatively, loops of cane or lacquered cords. There is similar coiling on the arms from wrist to elbow.

The regional costumes of the men show very little change from the basic longyi and jacket. Often on the left hip is carried a large, coloured cotton or canvas bag as the costume has no pockets. In the remote mountainous regions of the north-west the men of the Naga tribe wear elaborate head-dresses which are made from bear's fur, the feathers of birds and the tusks of the boar. They also use tufts of animal hair and wear necklaces of beads and tigers' teeth. For dancing there is a very elaborate longyi worn with a white eingyi jacket and a small white headscarf tied in a knot with a bow at the back. Sometimes calf-length trousers are worn and the longyi is draped at the waist. White stockings are worn with or without sandals.

NEW ZEALAND

The Maoris settled mainly on the north island of New Zealand and developed an unique culture and civilisation.

Using flax fibre they devised what is known as 'finger weaving' or Taniko; two sticks were placed in the ground and the top of the garment or the border to be woven was suspended between them. The fibre yarns had been dyed black, yellow or a reddish brown and were knotted together with unbleached fibres to form Taniko patterns. The dyes were obtained from various trees; black was made by steeping the fibres in a solution made from bruised bark followed by immersion in mud for several days.

The patterns on the clothing were always geometrical and those carved on wood, circular or spiral; all the patterns had names and meanings. A common design is a downward zig-zag pattern denoting the path of the sea.

Many of the traditional designs have been replaced by modern patterns and the use of flax in Taniko has been replaced by wool and cotton which is worked on to canvas.

Women and girls wear a pari or bodice made in a taniko design. The piupiu skirt is worn by both sexes and it is made from flax which has been treated and dyed and formed into tight rolls. The women's piupiu is mid-calf in length and the men's comes to just above the knees. The women wear a headband which is called a tipare and the men wear a body band which is called a tatua; both bands are made in taniko.

Feather cloaks are much admired and considered one of the most beautiful of the Maori traditional garments. The finest cloaks are worn by the chiefs and nobles. These cloaks consist of white feathers from a wood pigeon's breast and green ones from its back. The bluish black feathers from the parson bird and red ones from parrots are also used. All these feathers were tied into the flax fibre base.

Maoris also tattooed their faces and this was considered by the women as a mark of manly beauty. The males would have the whole of the face covered in circular patterns, but the women had only the lips and the chin tattooed.

The Maori costumes shown in Plate 66 are now only worn by folk groups on festive occasions.

CANADA

Wherever the Indians settled in Canada they adapted themselves to their environment and made full use of the natural resources available. The tribes on the Pacific coast made use of the cedar trees for building houses and the bark was used in the making of costumes. Spruce was woven into a material for the making of hats used in bad weather.

The people of the Plains were buffalo hunters and the animal skins were used for both their tents and for clothing. In the east the bark of trees was used for wigwams and animal skins for clothing. In the north the Eskimos responded to the demands made by the climate and made protective clothing from the skins of caribou and seals.

It was the French who first colonised the shores of the St. Lawrence and finding themselves ill-equipped to meet the climatic conditions were greatly helped by the Indians who taught them how to make moccasins, fur mittens and clothing from buckskin.

The early Indian costumes were mainly based on the wrap-around skirt, an apron or breechclout (a type of loin cloth), leggings, cloaks and the poncho type of cape and shirts.

The Indians decorated their costumes with designs made from beads, woven braid, animal fur, quills and feathers. Each tribe had its own designs revealing identity and area. Patterns were inspired by environment and there were strong links with the natural world: trees, mountains and various animals were incorporated into geometric shapes. The Indians held strong beliefs in supernatural power and thought that by the wearing of animal skins, feathers and claws, the strength and courage of the animal could be passed on to the wearer.

Beadwork is very popular among Indians and the tribes of the east coast used conch and clam shells to form beads. Inland, beads were made from stones, minerals and bones. The colours of the beads changed according to the area and tribe and, with the coming of the Europeans, designs began to change. By the late seventeenth century costumes became more ornate, with the use of embroidery and glass beads (obtained from the exchange of furs) and the use of appliqué work. Floral designs were used, especially by the Woodland tribes round the Great Lakes. It is thought that these designs were influenced by the embroidered vestments of the missionaries.

European traders also introduced silver coins, woollen blankets, mirrors, metal needles, thimbles and the use of iron tools. Waistcoats and shirts were worn by the men, and the women, who had previously worn skirts, now began to wear dresses with sleeves. By the nineteenth century many of the costumes had become very elaborate.

Plate 67 shows a Tlingit Indian. He is a Kwakiutl from British Columbia and is dressed for a ceremonial dance in a Chilkat blanket and wooden mask. The mask represents a raven, an important part of Indian mythology. The blanket is made from mountain goat wool woven on shredded cedar bark; the design is first painted on to a pattern board by a man and then woven by a woman. The name for the blanket in Tlingit is 'the dancing fringe', because of the long woollen border.

Originally the black dye was obtained from hemlock, the yellow colour from lichen and the blue-green from copper. Modern blankets are made from chemical dyes and wool.

Underneath the blanket he wears a decorated tunic, apron and leggings.

Although the Europeans influenced the Indian form of dress, they had little contact with the Inuit or Eskimo. Their form of dress has changed very little and is still based on the original standard design of tunic and trousers. The long-sleeved jacket, known as a parka, kooletah, amouti or atigi, is made from the skins of the caribou. In the summer these jackets are made from a thick cloth or duffle material. The parka is usually embroidered round the hem and the sleeves with floral or geometric patterns, depending upon the region. Strips of highly coloured embroidered braid are also used for decoration and placed according to the individual taste of the wearer. Some groups appliqué strips of sealskin on to their parkas. Caribou hide is prepared by removing the hair from one side with a special knife. At one time the hides were smoked but are now often stretched on frames and bleached and dried in the sun. Women and girls favour white parkas: in the far north and especially for winter wear, the fur is not removed in order to gain added warmth and protection. During the winter men and women wear several layers of underclothes, but the looseness of the clothing worn helps to insulate the body on the same principle as that of the Arabs, whose loose clothing gives them coolness. Plate 67 illustrates an Eskimo woman.

In the summer months, when the daylight can last for twenty-four hours a day, the women wear cotton dresses under their parkas. The men and children wear lighter weight trousers. On Sundays it was customary for the men to wear white duffle trousers replacing those made from polar bear skin.

Both men and women wear boots called mukluks, being made from sealskin and into which the trousers are tucked. After being scraped, stretched and dried, the skin would become very hard and had to be chewed for several hours before it became soft enough for stitching! Different parts of the seal were used in the making of mukluks and caribou sinew for the stitching. The soles have to be replaced about every three months, depending upon the amount of wear. The hide from the seal's flipper is the most hardwearing. Women wear red or blue woollen stockings and thick mittens are worn by everyone.

Immigrants from most European countries have settled in Canada and the traditional customs of these ethnic groups has always been encouraged within the Canadian environment. The wearing of folk costumes and the performing of various songs and dances plays an important part in Canadian life today.

U.S.A.

Early groups of migrants in North America soon adapted themselves to their local physical environments and developed specific cultures which formed the basis of the many ethnic Indian tribes. In the U.S.A. there are roughly five different areas in which they settled, with an overlap into Canada and Mexico. They are: The Eastern Woodlands, the Great Plains, the South-West, the Plateau and Great Basin, and the North Pacific Coast. Within these areas were seven major groups and numerous tribes.

The man's basic garment was the breechclout, a type of loin cloth made from deer or buffalo skin. Some tribes wore a short square apron which covered the front and back. These were decorated with tribal designs. With the breechclout long leggings were worn reaching to the tops of the thighs and made from soft leather and later from cloth. These leggings were basically used for protection against the weather and in hunting, as well as for ceremonial purposes. The outside edges of the leggings were decorated with braid or fringed.

Plate 69 illustrates the work costume of the Woodland tribes which allows more freedom of movement than the elaborate ceremonial dress. He wears an apron rather than the more popular breechclout as this is a feature of these tribes. The apron is decorated with a design made with small beads.

A form of shirt called 'a war shirt' was worn by many tribes and was a garment used for ceremonial purposes rather than for war. Made from buckskin they were decorated with braid, beadwork, tufts of horsehair (and sometimes human hair) or animal skins or fur.

The Woodland tribe wore very distinctive shirts, black in colour with black leggings and aprons, all decorated with floral designs. Short capes and decorated yokes made from buckskin or the thick brown fur of the bear were worn by the North-East tribes. Waistcoats were probably copied from those worn by the European traders. Chokers, ties, cuffs and gauntlets are all modern additions. The fringed gauntlets were probably copied from those worn by the U.S. cavalry.

A very striking part of the Indian costume is the magnificent feathered head-dress. First worn by the Plains tribes, it was later adopted by tribes in other areas. Made from eagles' feathers, it had great significance. The eagle is a bird much admired for its beauty and strength and a feather

229

from this bird could be worn only after a very brave deed had been carried out. For very exceptional deeds more than one feather would be allotted, or a feather marked in a special way.

The head of a tribe or very brave warriors who earned a great many feathers, would wear a single or double row of feathers down the back. Plains and Woodland Indians wore an interesting head-dress called 'The Roach'. This was made from dyed horsehair and shaped like a crest. It was attached to a decorated head harness and topped by a single feather (see Plate 69).

There are numerous head-dresses amongst the various tribes, many being worn only on ceremonial occasions or for dances; often these head-dresses would represent buffaloes or eagles. The Iroquois and other eastern tribes wore round, tight-fitting caps of skin or feathers decorated with plumes.

The Indians protected their feet with moccasins, a shoe adopted by the early settlers who found them more suitable for the terrain than the heavy European boot. The moccasin can be made in two ways, either with a firm hard sole of thick buffalo rawhide or with a soft leather sole.

The Indians of the South-West and the Plains wore the hard soled moccasins for protection against the stony ground and the cacti: the Woodland tribes needed a more flexible shoe which suited the forest country and was ideal for hunting and canoeing. Early Indians and some tribes on the north-west coast and the southern plains went barefooted.

Each tribe made and decorated their moccasins in slightly different ways: if an Indian scout found a discarded shoe he was able to tell which tribe it was that had passed that way. The Apache men wore a moccasin made like a boot with the upper part used as a protective covering round the calf. When this was not needed it could be turned down and used as a pocket in which to carry small objects. Short calf leggings were also worn by other tribes, but were separate and not joined to the moccasin.

The women's costume followed a similar pattern of style and development to that of the man. From a short, wrap-around skirt (which is still to be found among the Indians of South America) it gradually changed into a loose one or two piece dress. Climatic conditions as well as contact with Europeans did much to bring about the changes. Originally their costumes were made from the skins of deer, elk or other animals and changed very little among the tribes. From a simple dress there gradually developed more elaborate garments with beadwork, shells and appliqué as added decoration. The dress for work was fairly simple, but for ceremonial occasions much more elaborate.

Plate 69 shows a woman who belongs to the Sioux Indian tribe; she is recognisable by the design across the yoke of her dress and on her moccasins. The long fringed dress is made of soft leather and round her lower legs and ankles she wears short leggings which act as a protection against animal and snake bites.

With the coming of the Europeans and the life in reservations forced upon the Indians, the women's dress changed and they wore full skirts and loose blouses made from cotton and calico and the use of skins for clothing ceased. Needles and thread were introduced and fibres made from animal sinews and the cactus thorn or bone needles were abandoned.

Necklaces have always been a feature of the Indian costume and these were made from shells, beads and braid woven with beads. In winter, blankets were wrapped round the body. The women's moccasins were made in the same pattern as those of the men.

With the discovery of North America, the colonists were attracted by the wealth of the New World. The majority of the immigrants were British, with a large Dutch settlement in the area which is now New York. The Spanish, attracted by the climate of California and Mexico, settled in those areas and the French stayed mainly in the Mississippi region. With this great expansion of the population and the development of the land by pioneers, a new type of costume emerged for the cowboy.

The Great Plains, which were the home of millions of bison or buffalo, were occupied by the Plains Indian tribes, whose way of life depended on the buffalo; they used the animals for food and buffalo skins for clothing and making tents. Soon, however, the Indians were driven out by the pioneer immigrants and cattle ranches appeared. It was then that the familiar figure of the North American cowboy first emerged.

In common with the cowboys of Central and South America, the costume evolved to suit the occupation. This consisted of a type of leather over-trouser, or 'chaps', leather jackets or waistcoats, bright shirts, a gunbelt, heeled boots with spurs and large, felt 'Stetson' hats.

The many folk dance groups which represent the U.S.A. wear the costumes based on early settlers. With considerable adaptation from earlier years, the women wear full-skirted, short-sleeved dresses in bright ginghams or spotted material with several petticoats underneath: with these dresses they wear low heeled leather shoes.

The men wear a cowboy style costume which consists of plain or striped trousers tucked into high boots, or the trousers can be worn with ordinary leather shoes. The bright cotton shirts are plain coloured or checked, with long sleeves, and there is either a knotted scarf or a knotted bow at the neck.

Plate 68 illustrates a couple dressed in modern square dance costumes. The colours and patterns of both the dress and the shirt can vary considerably.

MEXICO

The introduction of European customs and of Christianity into Mexico was never fully accepted by the indigenous Indians who blended their own strong culture with that of their Spanish conquerors. This is revealed in Mexican music, dance, design and costumes.

In the various regions there are numerous costumes to be seen and the variations are created by the purpose for which they are being worn, for example, work, fiestas, religious processions and dancing. The ancient cultures are seen in these costumes and in the more isolated areas women still spin and weave in the same way as before the Spanish conquest. Cotton thread or henequen fibre is spun on an old form of spindle and distaff. Lengths of material are woven on primitive looms consisting of a lengthways warp being stretched between two sticks.

Many of the designs and embroidery used today are of stylised birds, animals, flowers and geometrical Indian patterns, each region having its own traditional designs; the patterns have strong links with the old Aztec and Mayan beliefs. Colours also had a significance as the empire was divided into four regions with red for the east, yellow for the south, black for the west and white for the north.

The women's costume is based on variations of a huipil and quechquemitl, a skirt and head-dress. The huipil is a type of tunic dress or shift, worn mainly in the south, and it can be long or short, narrow or full in size and can be made from wool or cotton. In Yucatan the huipil is white with flowers embroidered on the square neckline and round the hems (see Plate 70). In Oaxaca, a region which has numerous costumes, an ankle-length white huipil has wide horizontal bands of decoration round the skirt. From the same region there is a white huipil which has flowers embroidered with brightly coloured silks down the front or a huipil dyed purple which is worn over a long white petticoat. Purple is a rare and much sought after dye which is obtained from the snail. There are huipils decorated with bands of pink and blue ribbons alternating with floral patterns or woven alternating stripes and geometric patterns. The quechquemitl is a type of triangular poncho which covers the upper body and is worn mostly in the northern and central regions. From the central region of San Luis Potosí there is a white quechquemitl embroidered with bright patterns and from the east one with broad coloured bands decorating the border. The quechquemitl can be worn with the points to the front and back or at the sides, according to the region of origin.

The Indians adopted the skirt and blouse from European dress and adapted them to their own costumes. Skirts are usually full and of varying lengths and colours, under which there are several petticoats. In Vera Cruz, on the Gulf of Mexico, for fiestas women wear long white cotton skirts ending in two or three layers of frills and with slight trains. Above the skirt is a white blouse, a white quechquemitl and a tiny black apron decorated with flowers.

Plate 71 shows the women's costume known as the china poblana. The decorated blouse is of white linen and is embroidered with silk thread or glass beads. The skirt, or zagalejo, is in two tones with a contrasting section at the waist and hem. The skirts can be very elaborate and decorated with coloured sequins, sometimes forming the country's emblem. The national colours of red, green and white are popular colours for this dress.

The Tehuana women from the state of Oaxaca wear very full skirts made in a dark coloured satin upon which are printed or embroidered large coloured flowers. These patterns are thought to have been inspired by the designs on the imported shawls from Spain. For the fiesta these skirts have a deep frill of white lace round the hem and are worn with a short matching huipil and an elaborate head-dress.

Blouses are coloured or white, usually with short sleeves. Many of the white blouses have embroidery on the sleeves and neckline.

An essential part of the women's costume is the stole or rebozo (see Plate 71). It developed from the need to cover the head in church as well as protection against the weather, apart from decoration. When slung from the shoulder it can be used for carrying a baby or the shopping. The rebozo are woven in bright colours and patterns or can be quite plain. The Tarascan women of Michoacán wear a black wool rebozo woven with fine narrow blue and white stripes, which is worn with a black skirt, a bright sash and a square-necked embroidered blouse.

Not all costumes have head-dresses, the rebozo being a substitute covering, but the hair is often elaborately dressed. One of the most elaborate head-dresses is worn by the women of Tehuana; made of white lace it frames the face and the shoulders. The manner of wearing this head-dress denotes whether the occasion is religious or social.

In Tlaxcaca, in the east, folded scarves are worn on the head or a half gourd, brightly painted, is tied on the head over a headscarf.

The men's costumes are based on the European style of white shirts and trousers, but vary according to region. The shirt can be worn tucked into the trousers and with a bright sash tied at the waist, or it can be worn outside the trousers like a jacket. This jacket-style shirt, or manta, can be buttoned to the neck or worn with a knotted scarf. The Nahua Indians from Puebla wear a loose-fitting, short-sleeved woollen tunic over their shirts. Known as a coton, this type of tunic is found in several regions, the Nahua wearing a deep purple one: in the Chiapas province they are in red and white stripes. The coton can be worn loose or belted.

In the Chiapas highlands, the men of the Tzotzil and Tzetzal tribes wear a type of tunic called a chamarra. This is a length of cotton material which has a hole for the head and when worn the folds are carefully draped and tied round the body. White shorts are worn underneath or, if from Tenejapa, they are red. The men from Huistan wear a type of baggy loin cloth instead of shorts. A feature of their costume are the sandals which are made with ankle guards at the back, a style which goes back to the Mayas.

Plate 70 illustrates one of the most colourful men's costumes found in Mexico: that of a Huichol Indian from Santa Catarina in the west. The costumes are made by the women and all the embroidery is in a cross stitch. The long tunic shirt, or rahuarero, and the wide trousers, or shaveresh, are both made from cotton. Several sashes are worn round the waist and the tuharra, or cape, is of red wool. On a waistband or belt called a cosihuire, are fastened small embroidered bags decorated with red tufts. Most Mexican Indians carry woven bags over their shoulders and the illustration shows one made in brown and white wool whilst the other is cotton and decorated in red as the cosihuire. The flat crowned, straw hat, or reporero, is decorated with balls of coloured yarn and from the brim hang butterfly cocoons. On his feet are leather sandals, or huaraches.

In the cold weather the men wear a woollen serape, not unlike a poncho but which opens down the front. When it is not in use it is folded and worn across the shoulders.

234

The men's costume most associated with Mexico is that of the charro or horseman's costume, the festive version of which is shown in Plate 71. In common with other cowboy costumes the design is both functional and decorative. The short jacket allows freedom of movement and the tight trousers give protection when in the saddle. The shirt is of white cotton or linen and a long silk bow is tied at the neck. Silver buttons and cord decorate the trousers. The belt has a silver buckle and the edge of the large sombrero is decorated with silver thread. Over the shoulder or carried on the saddle there will be a colourful serape. His riding boots have slightly raised heels. This costume is in fine woollen cloth but the working one is often in soft light brown leather.

GUATEMALA

With a strong Indian majority, the way of life in Guatemala is very different from its neighbouring Central American countries.

Living in the highlands and in the many villages around Lake Atitlán, the Indians wear their costumes as part of everyday life and not just for fiestas or special occasions. They have a love of colour and pattern and each village has its own specially woven designs.

Cotton and wool are the main materials used and in Salcajá, a village in the Lake Atitlán region, material known as jaspé is woven. The yarn is first dyed and then the warps stretched by wrapping them round the modern telephone poles. Red is a very popular dye. Until the introduction of chemical dyes in the nineteenth century, Guatemala exported large amounts of cochineal and indigo, the source of reds, blues, purples and pinks which, together with green and orange, are the colours found in many of the costumes.

The women's costumes are based on long, ankle-length skirts which are woven or embroidered in stripes and various patterns. Green and purple wool is used in embroidery and the designs show stylised birds, people, stripes or rhythmic geometrical designs which come from the ancient Mayan culture. The skirts are narrow and sometimes have a gathered section. The old looms and manner of weaving produced material in a narrow width, which governed the cut of the costume.

A type of loose blouse called a huipil, which has various styles, colours and patterns, is worn. Sashes with woven designs are tied round the waist and a long scarf, or rebozo, is draped over one shoulder. Turbans are worn with most costumes and these range from a simple band to very elaborate styles; they are predominantly red in colour. The women from Santiago, a village on Lake Atitlán, wear turbans which resemble halos. A long, narrow, red band about eleven metres long has each end embroidered to the depth of a metre with geometrical patterns in orange, green and purple. The band is wound round the head with the hair specially arranged to give the required halo effect. (Plate 72 illustrates a girl in the working costume of this village.)

At Zunil, a little village situated between two volcanoes, the women weave and wear large purple cloaks, the colour signifying the eventual eruption of the volcanoes and the destruction of the villages.

The men's costumes are equally colourful, the trousers are usually calf-length, loose fitting and made in a variety of colours ranging from plain white to striped patterns in reds, pinks, blues, black and white. Multi-coloured, long-sleeved, striped shirts are tucked into the trousers and a sash is worn. In some villages the men wear jackets embroidered in bright coloured wools. Sashes and trousers are embroidered or woven with animal or quetzal bird designs, or in pink or purple stripes. Floral designs are not used extensively.

The men from the village of San Antonio in the Lake Atitlán region, wear a black and white checked skirt, which reaches from the waist to mid-thigh, over their brightly striped trousers and shirt. Plate 72 shows a boy who is a farm worker from the Sololá region. In the village of San Juan the men wear loose tunic coats reaching to the knees and split up the sides, thus forming a type of apron. A red sash is tied round the waist and a red striped shirt is worn. The trousers are white. Many of the men carry a decorated canvas bag slung from the shoulder or tied round the waist. Hats range from the flat brimmed Panama style to round crowned hats with narrow brims, these being decorated with coloured hatbands and ribbons. Both men and women either go barefooted or wear a type of sandal.

HONDURAS

The costumes of Honduras are based on the style which was popular in the mid-19th century and have much in common with their neighbouring countries. Although European dress is worn mostly in the towns and cities, the local costumes are still popular in the villages, especially during fiesta times.

The women's dress changes according to region and occasion. For work it is very plain with simple coloured trimming and is made in calico or cotton. The Sunday and fiesta dresses are made of silk or cotton, embroidered with silk using old Mayan patterns and designs. For work a short white skirt has an added frill round the hem and is decorated with a band of coloured braid or coloured stitching. With this skirt is worn a white blouse with short puff sleeves, a round 'boat' neckline and a deep frill, a pattern which is very popular in so many central American countries. The older women prefer a similar dress, but with a longer skirt and the blouse has a wider frill but no sleeves. The little girl illustrated in Plate 72 wears this everyday costume.

The more elaborate style of dress has a skirt with two layers of frills, a long-sleeved blouse with a high neckline and a deep frill round the shoulders. Another style of dress, worn either short or long, depending upon the occasion, has a blouse with elbow-length sleeves ending in frills and an inset front panel decorated with coloured braid: the skirt follows the usual pattern. Several strings of beads are worn, which have the local name of lageimas de San Pedro. The beads are made from dried seeds and thorns, which are painted in bright colours. The hair is usually worn in two plaits and the ends tied with bright ribbons. Open sandals are the usual form of footwear.

The men wear the typical costume of long white trousers, long-sleeved, white tunic shirts worn outside the trousers and red handkerchiefs tied round the neck. Straw hats are worn and the sandals are similar to those worn by the women.

COSTA RICA

In the women's costumes of Costa Rica there are found several variations, but all are based on the frilled blouse and full skirt. In the regions bordering on Nicaragua the skirts tend to be narrow, but those nearer to Panama have fuller skirts, not unlike the pollera. For working the skirts are shorter, but longer styles are worn for galas etc. The skirts vary in colour and range from white to a multi-coloured effect. Plate 72 shows a woman wearing a full skirt with a deep basque cut in a zig-zag pattern.

The white blouses are made with round, boat shaped necklines and have one, two or three frills embroidered in floral silk designs. For galas, the frills are more elaborately embroidered.

A coloured stole, or rebozo, is draped round the shoulders or over the head. There is usually a cross, medallion or locket suspended from a black band round the neck and circular golden ear-rings recall the Indian tradition. Lightweight shoes or sandals are mostly worn.

The most popular costume for the man consists of black or dark brown long trousers worn with a long-sleeved white shirt and a red knotted handkerchief at the neck (see Plate 73). A coloured sash is tied round the waist and a long knife in a decorated leather sheath hangs from a silver chain worn over the sash. He wears a straw Panama hat and either sandals or western style shoes.

For work in the plantations, the long trousers are replaced by serviceable and comfortable shorts or there can be a form of skirt or kilt. With these are worn a white or coloured shirt outside the trousers.

PANAMA

One of the most beautiful costumes to be found in Central and South America is the women's pollera from Panama. This costume, which is made in cotton, has a very full, long skirt, a blouse top with short sleeves and a boat neckline draped with frills. The pollera is thought to have come from Spain, the loose skirt and blouse once worn by the slaves or servants.

There are three styles of pollera, the one from the Los Santos province being the most elaborate (illustrated in Plate 74). This costume is made in fine white cotton and covered with embroidery, Valencian lace and the locally made Mundizzo lace. The costume from the provinces of Herrera and Veraquas are similar in style but without the embroidery and are made in pastel shades as well as white. The skirt has three tiers, unlike the Los Santos costume which has only two. Several chains are worn round the neck and also ear-rings. The hair is worn in two plaits and tied with ribbons and several gold-topped combs are placed in the sides and the back of the head. Through the teeth of the combs coloured woollen threads are woven and tied across the forehead. When the hair is dressed without the combs, a white, small brimmed straw hat is worn.

A much simpler pollera is used for everyday wear, called the Montuna or diaria. This has a full skirt made in two or three tiers and is in floral patterned cotton. The white or pastel coloured blouse is in the same design, but without an upper frill. The plaited hair is tied with ribbons and a white straw hat is worn.

With each costume a black velvet ribbon with a cross, coin or medallion attached, is worn round the neck. White shoes with low heels are usually worn with the pollera de gala from Los Santos, but for everyday wear an ordinary lightweight shoe or sandal is worn. The men's costume consists of two styles, one to accompany the women's gala dress and one for everyday wear. The dress or formal Camisella style has a white, long-sleeved, cotton shirt with a little stand-up collar. The front and back of the shirt is decorated with a row of fine tucks or open-work embroidery. The shirt is worn outside dark blue or black trousers and the lightweight shoes are made of white canvas and leather. A shallow brimmed straw hat is worn.

The Montuna or country-style fiesta costume is similar in pattern, but the shirt and trousers are made in a heavy white cotton or linen. The long-sleeved shirt has a flat collar and a plain front, but the hem is fringed. The trousers reach only to the knees. For a fiesta the shirt is embroidered in petit point. Mostly the workers are barefooted or a home-made leather sandal is worn.

Numerous festivals and religious processions are held, during which fantastic and colourful costumes are worn, many of which represent good or bad devils.

CUBA

In Cuba the Spanish influence is dominant: the costumes have a similarity to those of other Latin American countries and a popular dress used in folk dance has the tight-fitting, hip length bodice with a full skirt gathered into the hip line rather than the waist. The boat or scooped neckline has a wide frill which covers the short sleeves.

A turban is tied round the head and often this is surmounted by a little straw hat. The dress is always in bright colours, made in cotton, and a white, spotted or pastel background is popular.

The men wear long trousers which can be rolled to the calf, and white is the usual colour. A loose shirt with long sleeves is worn outside the trousers and stripes or checks are popular as patterns.

Straw or felt hats with broad brims protect the head from the sun and lightweight shoes or sandals are worn by both men and women, although they are often barefooted when they are dancing.

In Plate 75 two dancers illustrate the Cuban costume.

239

COLOMBIA

The costumes of Colombia tend to reflect the climate and landscape. In the mountain regions wool and dark colours are used, but towards the coast, where the climate becomes tropical and there is a profusion of flowers, cotton is the material generally used.

The women's skirts are ankle or calf length and are made in black, brown or dark blue wool. Blouses are more colourful and are in white, coloured or flowered cotton. For special occasions, a white blouse with a boat shaped neckline is decorated with two layers of white lace which forms a large round collar. These blouses have elbow length sleeves ending in frills or cuffs. The blouses are frequently hidden by large black or dark coloured, fringed shawls which are worn like capes over the head. Plate 76 illustrates the version of this costume worn in the region of Bogotá.

In common with all Andean people, felt hats are worn by men, women and children, and the hats are in black or brown, shaped like trilbies and worn pulled down over the eyes. Straw hats can also be worn. Many of the women go barefooted, but alpargatas, or sandals, made from a coarse cotton canvas are also worn.

The men also wear dark clothes with jackets and trousers of the same colour. Over these are worn a type of poncho or cape called a ruana, which are made in wool and ranges from oatmeal to black in colour, these colours being the natural shades of the wool. Similar to those of the women, the hats are felt and the sandals, if worn, are made of canvas.

A famous area of Colombia is the Llanos, a vast plain and known as a large cattle producing area. The cattle are tended by tough cowboys known as Llaneros; the riding costume worn by these men is illustrated by the man on the left in Plate 76.

VENEZUELA

With the discovery of oil in 1917, Venezuela became the richest of all the South American countries. Thousands of European immigrants poured into the country to work on the expansion programme and consequently many of the old traditional ways and also costumes were lost. Today the playing of national music is encouraged however, especially the rhythmical Joropos, and the costumes show a strong similarity to other South American countries.

The women wear short-sleeved blouses with a boat or scoop neckline decorated with a frill. A full knee or calf length skirt is gathered into a waistband. The hair is worn in two plaits and is tied or plaited with a coloured ribbon. Straw hats with turned-up brims or long scarves are worn on the head.

Cotton is used for the costumes and on special occasions the blouse and skirt are in white or pastel shades of blue, yellow or pink. An everyday costume has a coloured skirt in a spotted or floral pattern. Spotted patterns are very popular, reflecting Spanish influence. A white blouse is usual for everyday wear, together with white or red shoes with small heels.

The men wear a loose, long-sleeved white shirt, worn outside the trousers, which are also white. This is the formal costume, but for work the trousers are rolled up to the calves and a short-sleeved, round-necked shirt is worn. Broad horizontal stripes are much favoured, with the coloured stripes against a white background. A coloured scarf is knotted at the neck and a straw hat with a turned-up brim is worn. The men are either barefooted, have sandals or wear formal shoes. Plate 76 shows a Venezuelan man in working costume.

BRAZIL

The population of Brazil embraces many different racial and ethnic groups; no definite costume has been established as people adapted their own national costumes to the climate and terrain of their new country.

One of the most colourful costumes worn is that of the Bahia women. Floral patterned, long cotton skirts and white blouses are worn with brightly striped turbans, stoles and numerous long necklaces of small coloured beads, all of which reflect their West African ancestry. Carnivals are very popular in Brazil, and many elaborate costumes are displayed, but these are mainly created for the occasion. The women's two piece costume with the frilly sleeved top, short flounced skirt and exaggerated turban does show an ethnic background.

Plate 77 shows a woman wearing a costume based on those worn by the early European colonists.

Two very large cattle breeding areas are found in the north-east and the south. A cattle ranchhand's life is a hard one and their costumes have been evolved to suit their way of life, much of which is spent in the saddle.

In the north-east the Vaqueiros or Boiadeiros (cowboys) roam the vast plains. These cowhands, accustomed to a hard life, wear a costume made entirely of leather, apart from a cotton shirt. Plate 77 shows this costume. The leather garments become hard from wear and act as a protection from the dangerous and sharp needles of the cacti.

The Gauchos who live in the south are very different in outlook, dress and physical appearance to the Vaqueiros, as the climate in the south is less harsh. Black or grey loose trousers are tucked into black leather boots; a sleeveless waistcoat is worn over a long-sleeved shirt and a long coloured scarf is tied round the neck. A black or grey felt hat with a wide brim is worn.

There are various Indian tribes whose way of life have not changed. They wear very little, but have a great sense of colour and create fantastic ceremonial head-dresses; these are made from natural materials such as feathers and leaves. They paint their bodies in intricate patterns and designs.

PERU

The art of weaving, dyeing and the use of colours and patterns, all showing strong Inca influence, are still in use in Peru today; it is also reflected with European influence in the costumes.

In Peru there is a very large Indian population who live mainly on the plateau and the mountainous regions. These communities are almost self-supporting, weaving their clothes from the alpaca, llama and sheep wool. The old form of belt or vertical weaving is still in use, a form used by the Incas.

The two main Indian groups are the Quecha and the Aymará.

The women wear full gathered, hand-woven skirts, black being the popular colour. It is unusual to find dark shades in South America, but the use of black has been attributed to mourning for the last Inca ruler. Black skirts are worn in the region of Cuzco as well as other loyalist areas. A touch of colour is introduced in the bright border of the hem and the trimming on the jackets. In the mountain regions the women favour blue or green skirts. For weddings the black and coloured skirts are replaced by red ones.

Skirts are worn one on top of the other and are all in different colours, which is very effective in dancing the huayno. The numerous skirts also give added warmth during the highland winters. White or brightly coloured blue or green long-sleeved blouses are worn, either separately or under jackets. A short cape or mantas is worn either round the shoulders or over the head, fastening under the chin. Made in a woollen material, it reflects Spanish influence.

A flat hat with a slightly turned-up brim is worn, either over the cape or manta or over the knitted helmet or chullo. Sometimes a felt hat is worn in black or light brown. One hat is often worn on top of another and they are seldom removed, except to sleep. If the hat has flowers in the band it means that the wearer requires a husband. Feet are bare or sandals are worn.

The men wear calf-length or long trousers, usually black and worn with a shirt, waistcoat or coat. Over a coloured sash a belt is sometimes fastened. A brightly coloured poncho or open serapes are an essential part of the costume. The headgear is the same as the women's, but the knitted chullo is worn with both styles of hat, especially in the winter. Bare feet or simple sandals are usual.

Plate 78 illustrates the men's and women's costumes from Peru.

For their celebrations and religious processions, special costumes are worn, highlighting the Indian's love of colour, as well as festivities.

BOLIVIA

More than half of the population of Bolivia are Indian and a third are Mestizo, a mixture of Indian and Spanish; the two main Indian groups are the Aymará and Quecha. Life is primitive and the mode of living and dress has changed very little over the years: many indications of the Inca civilisation are still evident.

For clothing cotton and wool are the main materials. The coarse, hard-wearing, woollen cloth is made from alpaca and llama wool.

The Indian's love of colour is shown in the women's bright skirts, or polleras, under which numerous coloured petticoats are worn. The skirts are in red, pink, light blue, dark or light green. A vividly coloured, long-sleeved blouse is worn outside the skirt and round the shoulders is worn a woollen cape or shawl. These are orange, pink, red or checked in colour and are often fringed. Bolivian babies are carried on their mother's backs in a blanket which is knotted in front and worn over the shawl. A feature of the costume is the bowler or derby hat. Made in felt, the wool is first soaked, pounded and then starched or moulded. The favourite colours for these hats are brown, beige, black and grey, all of which are the natural colours of the wool. Occasionally white is worn, but white llama pelts are rare and valuable and, consequently, saleable. The bowler hats are always removed when the women enter church. Plate 78 shows an Aymará Indian from one of the many villages round Lake Titicaca wearing this costume.

The other form of hat is made of white straw and is shaped like a top hat or similar to the hats worn by Welsh women. These are very popular in Cochabamba. Large ponchos are worn and replace the capes.

Men wear dark trousers which reach either to the calf or to the ankle. Round the waist is a sash or belt and in summer sleeveless waistcoats in bright colours are worn over a shirt, and always a felt or straw hat. In the colder regions and in winter, the vividly woven poncho is worn. The poncho is a piece of material with a hole for the head. Also popular is the serape, which is similar to the poncho, but has an opening in the front. In some regions white linen, calf-length trousers are worn with a short poncho in bright red, yellow and black stripes. A woven pocket or pouch with a fringed edge hangs from the waist.

A very popular form of headgear is a knitted or woven, tight-fitting helmet called a llucho or chullo. This can be plain, patterned in a geometrical design or ornamented with round suns and stylised llamas. It can be extremely cold in the high Altiplano area and this type of cap with its long earflaps is essential for warmth. A felt hat is worn over this if necessary.

Both men and women go barefooted or wear a home-made leather open sandal.

The Bolivians have a great love of carnivals at which the most colourful and elaborate costumes are worn.

PARAGUAY

The colonisation of Paraguay by the Spaniards was not extensive and the Paraguayans have retained many Guarani characteristics.

The women wear a dress which shows a strong Spanish background and which is similar in style to those found in other South American countries. Full cotton skirts made in bright colours are worn over white petticoats. For everyday wear the skirt is simple and is often made with the gathers or fullness coming from a tight-fitting basque which reaches

244

from the waist to the hips, a style worn by Spanish flamenco dancers. Plate 79 shows this everyday costume.

On Sundays or festive occasions skirts are more elaborate with one or two deep frills round the hem in contrasting colours. The Paraguayans have a love of colour and reds, blues, pinks and bright primary colours all create a vivid effect.

Blouses vary in style, with the round boat neck being very popular, and there are short puff sleeves, loose sleeves which reach to the elbows or long tight sleeves. The neckline is decorated with embroidery or a deep frill. Blouses can be in white cotton or of the same material and colour as the skirt, or in a contrasting shade.

Straw hats have round crowns and large flat brims and at fiesta time these are decorated with flowers or painted in bright floral patterns. Silver necklaces are very popular, both with old and young. Sandals or European heeled shoes are the usual form of footwear.

The men when working on the cattle ranches wear the typical cowboy dress of full, baggy trousers, either in black or brown, which are tucked into boots of a similar colour. White shirts are worn with long sleeves and a white scarf is tied at the neck. A striped or red poncho is worn or folded and carried over one shoulder. On Sundays a more elaborate shirt is worn with embroidery down the front and the everyday straw hat is replaced by a broad brimmed felt hat with a chin strap. Boots can also be elaborate and are decorated with leather work. A buckle and strap keeps the top of the boot secure. Round the ankle the leather is pleated, a feature of Paraguayan boots, allowing more freedom and comfort for the feet. Working boots are simple with a minimum of decoration.

Another type of costume is based on a long-sleeved shirt worn with ankle length trousers and boots. This is for those working on the land rather than cattle men. The shirt can be white, blue, dark blue or black, made in cotton, and can be quite plain or embroidered and decorated for special occasions. Straw hats usually accompany this costume.

CHILE

The population of Chile mainly consists of Indians, European immigrants and mestizo, or mixed races. The Indian tribes constitute a high percentage of the population, of which one of the main groups are the Araucanians.

The costume follows a similar pattern to that of other South

American countries, with an adaptation of the western style of dress. The feature of the women's costume is the wearing of a long piece of material called a manto, which is draped over the head, round the face, neck and shoulders in various ways. This form of head-dress can be worn over European dress or the full Indian skirts.

The Araucanians, who live in the southern provinces, weave their own material for clothing. The wool is dyed, red and dark blue being the most popular colours. The costumes have full skirts over which is worn a long-sleeved jacket or blouse. Wrapped round the shoulders and knotted in front is a shawl or blanket, or sometimes a long woollen mantle, or ichella.

A silver chain necklace hung with silver coins is very popular; known as a tupu, the shape and design is based on those worn by the Incas. Felt or straw hats are worn, but on festive days there are silver head-dresses hung with coins and tied in front with green bows.

The Chilean cowboy or huaso wears a costume similar to the style found in other South American countries although there are slight individual differences which give a distinctive appearance. The huaso wears long black gaiters or leggings, not unlike those worn by Almagro and his band of Spanish followers who first invaded the country. Sandals are very popular with both men and women, although often they go barefooted.

Black, brown or pin-striped trousers are tucked into long black leather leggings or gaiters. The leggings are worn over a black boot or shoe and reach well over the knees. They are fastened with buckles at the sides and round the knees are tied bands from which hang long leather tassels. Under the square shaped, striped poncho or chamanto are worn a jacket and white shirt. Silver spurs are worn, and the round felt hat has a chin strap.

ARGENTINA

Argentina became prosperous in the nineteenth century with the development of the cattle industry. This expansion attracted Spanish and Italian immigrants, and also sheep farmers from England, Scotland and Wales.

The Argentinian women's dress is simple and is based on the pioneering style of a cotton or calico skirt and jacket. The ankle length, full skirt had a frill at the hem and the long-sleeved jacket had a frilled basque. A large apron was worn for work and a shawl was draped round the shoulders.

It is the man's costume which predominates and is as worn by the cowboys or gauchos who ride the vast pampas plains. The gauchos wore clothes which evolved for horse riding and showed the Indians' love of silver and colour for decoration. Baggy cotton trousers or bombachas were tucked into boots or buttoned at the ankles. Round the waist was a belt called a rastra made of silver coins.

The jacket fastens with silver buttons and a shirt is also worn. An indispensible part of the costume is the poncho, an all-purpose garment styled like a cape or cloak. Made of sheep wool, it is dyed in various colours and used as a blanket or for protection against the weather. On special occasions an apron is worn, called a chiripa; this can be plain or striped and consists of a wide length of coarse woollen cloth or flannel which is draped round the body and tucked into a belt or sash. Plate 80 shows the type of costume that would be worn on festive occasions. White linen or cotton loose trousers with decorated lace hems are worn.

A black or white wide-brimmed felt hat is worn and tight fitting riding boots, sometimes with silver spurs.

For working on the land, baggy trousers are worn with either a short boot or a type of sandal, called ushutas, made of rawhide or woven grass and not unlike a Spanish alpargata or the Italian ciocie.

There are many groups of Indians, such as the Guaranis in the north and the Pampas in the south and Patagonia. Their love of colour is shown in their woven garments and the silver ear-rings and brooches.

URUGUAY

In the nineteenth century large numbers of Italians and Spaniards came to settle in Uruguay. A new culture developed and new costumes evolved, especially for the women, based on the European styles. Today folk costumes are worn only on special occasions or for folk dancing and musical presentations.

The women wear long dark, cotton skirts, gathered at the waist, under which are white petticoats. Blouses are short sleeved and cut with a boat neckline; usually of white cotton or fine linen, coloured ones are worn on special occasions. A working costume would be in white and the only touch of colour would be a sash at the waist. The pioneering women had little time for elaborate costumes or head-dresses. The hair was plaited in two braids or made into a bun. Married women wore handkerchiefs tied under the chin. The women wore either a sandal or a lightweight shoe.

The men adapted the popular costume of the gauchos or cowboys, modelled on the style found in Argentina and other neighbouring countries. For work, loose white trousers were tucked into soft leather boots, but for special occasions the trousers, which ended in white lace frills, were worn outside the boots. A type of red skirt called a chiripá was worn over these trousers and this reached from waist to calf. It was originally split up the middle, but later became much fuller, similar to a divided skirt worn over the white trousers. Red and black were mainly used with a contrasting border. With the introduction of modern saddles, the gauchos gave up wearing the chiripá. Still worn in some of the rural areas are the full, baggy, bombachas trousers in blue, black, white or grey: loose sleeveless waistcoats are also worn over white, open-necked shirts with a white or black knotted scarf round the neck. A broad leather belt trimmed with silver coins or studs, or a deep woven belt is often worn. This helps support the back during the long hours in the saddle.

The boots are of soft leather rather then the hard, high-heeled style found among the gauchos in other countries. The cattle breeding areas are very flat, quite devoid of mountains and the gauchos need to stand in the saddle to scan the distances.

A white band used to be tied round the head over which was worn a white or black felt hat with a tall crown, but narrow brim. A chin strap keeps the hat in place. The modern gaucho no longer wears the protective white head band but wears a wider brimmed hat.

Plate 80 shows a horseman from Uruguay dressed for work.

ACKNOWLEDGEMENTS

The author would like to thank the following who have kindly supplied material and illustrations and given up valuable time in which to discuss costumes:

Helen Wingrave, Harry Goss, Dr V. Knivett, Marjorie Barton, Doreen Bird, Roderych Lange, Betty Harvey, Joseph Hanna Khoury, Robert Ernest, Aruba Coghlan, Dale Hyde, the Viltis magazine and V. Beliajus, and the Ontario Folkdance magazine.

Also many thanks are due to the Tourist and Information Offices of: The Netherlands, Malta, Czechoslovakia, Iran, Morocco, Tunisia, Iraq, Brazil, Honduras, India, Thailand, Japan and New Zealand, together with the Ceylon Tourist Board, The Tibet Society and the German Library.

INDEX

The numbers in italics refer to the colour plate illustrations. Other numbers are page references.